~~Frank S. MacShane~~

~~Fall Semester~~

~~Christmas,~~ 1942.

J. D. Thomas '56

GARZ-I

By

A VICTORIAN AT BAY

BY

ANNE KIMBALL TUELL

Author of

Mrs. Meynell and her Literary Generation

BOSTON

MARSHALL JONES COMPANY · Inc.

MDCCCXXXII

THE PLIMPTON PRESS · NORWOOD · MASSACHUSETTS

PRINTED IN THE UNITED STATES OF AMERICA

PREFACE

THESE essays have been, with few exceptions, revised from previous printing, and are here republished by permission of the periodicals in which they first appeared. Thanks for the courtesy are here offered to the *Atlantic Monthly*, the *Bookman*, the *Catholic World*, the *Contemporary Review*, the *Nation, Scribner's Magazine*, the *Sewanee Review*, the *South Atlantic Quarterly*, and to Henry Holt and Company, former publishers of the *Unpopular Review*. The author is gratefully indebted besides for kind suggestion and for recollections of their father to the daughters of T. E. Brown. The essay entitled "The Escape from Narcissus" was finished in a more elaborate form before the publication in the *Atlantic Monthly* of "The Professor and the Detective" by Miss Marjorie Nicolson and was withheld at the time because of the similarity in material.

Acknowledgment of kind permission to make brief quotation from copyright material is here made: to The Macmillan Company for excerpts from the poetry of T. E. Brown and of Christina Rossetti, from the *Letters* of Edward Fitzgerald and the *Letters* of Sir Walter Raleigh, from *The Renaissance* by Walter Pater and from *George Meredith* by J. B. Priestley; to Charles Scribner's Sons for selections from the works of George Meredith, *Poems, Richard Feverel, Beauchamp's Career,* and from *Studies from Ten Literatures* by Ernest Boyd; to E. P. Dutton and Company for passages from the *Letters* of T. E. Brown and from *And Even Now* by Max Beerbohm; to Curtis Brown, TD., for brief selections from works of Max Beerbohm, *Yet Again, Seven Men, A Variety of Things, Around Theatres;* to Little, Brown and Company for passages from the works of Henryk Sienkiewicz, *Sielanka, Children of the Soil, The Deluge,* translated by Jeremiah Curtin, and *Whirlpools* translated by Max A. Drexmal; to Harcourt, Brace and Company for sentences from *Messages* by Ramon Fernandez; to Methuen and Company for a passage of *The Sacred Wood* by T. S. Eliot; to Longmans, Green and Company for passages from *The Idea of a University* by John Henry Newman.

Wellesley College, 1932

CONTENTS

CRITIQUES

CROTCHETS

CRITIQUES

I

GEORGE MEREDITH

I

IT is comfortable to feel that George Meredith has
been slowly coming into style again in certain
quarters. The enthusiast has had cold company these
many years. Disillusion has been, as usual, partly
personal, as we have got from closer biographical
contacts more of the valet point of view. An excellent
genius is always smaller than the children of his
brain, and we hate to find out the fact. The gentle
reader dislikes to know that Meredith was speaking
bald truth when he pointed to himself as source of
The Egoist, that he knew of sentimental tailordom at
first hand and fashioned subtle snobberies out of
self-knowledge. The limitations of Meredith, besides,
now that reaction has given clarity to see them by,
bristle like a brush, and like a brush rubbed the
wrong way cause excessive irritation. The letters were
always disappointing: they have never warmed our
knowledge, but sound sometimes, as do the poorest
of the novels, like a noisy and apparently efficient
dynamo at work without the proper results of light
and heat. Sir Walter Raleigh set distaste at the
strongest: " A plain human situation and its obvious
meaning is nothing to him till he can dress it in its

brain vanities. He lived much alone and was certainly incapable of simple human intercourse. His letters shocked me — an oldish man writing like a conceited jackanapes." Mr. T. S. Eliot some years ago assumed airily that the whole vogue was worse than dead: " The Charles Louis Philippes of English literature are never done with because there is no one to kill their reputations; we still hear that Meredith is a master of prose and even a profound philosopher." But the general reaction has been less against Meredith than against lack of measure in critical adulation.

Returning favour is still playing very safe. Even Mr. Priestley, whose cautious praises gave courage to the faint-hearted, earned his moderate indulgences by a preliminary lay-out of condemnation which gave some concern to solicitous heirs of Meredith's memory. Meredith lacks, we are reminded, any power over ordinary relations and things; his narrative exists only for the scene; there is disproportionate emphasis on unimportant characters; the bulk of his characters are not created, not even constructed. But, the commination service well over, we hear that Meredith " contrived somehow to enlarge the whole scope of art."

Most of us will not go back to the superlatives of our first enthusiasm. In 1909, year of the novelist's death, *Life* did the present writer the honour to laugh at a certain passage on Meredith's work published in the *Atlantic Monthly:* " Wherein lies the intrinsic power to maintain its greatness despite the chill of dangerous self-knowledge? For, try as we will, to criticize his work, we find ourselves bound to pay it the compliment of large comparisons. It is impossible to liken Meredith to anything small. Perhaps his style is more obscure than Browning's, or his plots lack the simplicity of Molière's. We sometimes go as far as to say that he fails of the robust vitality of Shakespeare. No mean condemnation certainly. To what then shall we turn for the unifying secret of Meredith's art, the saving grace which keeps it forever above the level of the mediocre and perpetually significant? " Let us join today by all means in the pleasant spirit of *Life's* amusement. We no longer need the old hieratic grandeur of phrase. But we suspect increasingly that our youthful ardours hit nearer the truth than our protective cautions. He who perceives a new planet swim into his ken sees it better as a planet than he will ever see it again. Later he may realize that the temperature must be low there, that commercial interests will probably never be able to exploit it. But our literary enthusiasms may not be blind. Rather maybe they have not yet gone blind. " O brave new world that has such people in it! " was a very good piece of criticism. Perhaps in a sense our first glimpse of a thing is also our last.

Our day of " philosophical criticism " recrudescent is the appropriate day for Meredith revivals. Meaning is certainly coming in again. We rebels have been long whispering to ourselves that the conscious findings of the human mind are as respectable and as significant as the unconscious, that human relevancies are as true as irrelevancies, that the normal may have its turn again when abnormalities have run thin. Slices of life, streams of consciousness, psychological symbols of Bergsonian time, all have been welcome. But the spectacle of humanity in charge is as edifying to critical sensibilities as the spectacle of the human mind adrift. And like the novel — the novelist. Meredith was always a maker of shapes and meanings.

His trouble to get a reading in his early years came indeed from his uncommon amount of meaning. He was a puzzle, being that infrequent thing among the elder novelists, the creator-critic. Novelists who have been critics in English have been frequent enough since Fielding's day, but the right and the left hand have worked together only casually. And " criticism of life " in any language has made a novelist less often than is usually supposed. At least the word that is able to make flesh of abstract material is not usually an English word. Meredith stood aloof, suspected, for we are realizing more his difference from his predecessors — most because he tried, whether or not he succeeded, to create life after his idea. Self-consciousness always runs the risk of artifice; but it is probably true of fiction, as has been said of personal morals, that the finest truth requires considerable self-consciousness. Meredith, as M. Ramon Fernandez puts it, " caused a current of concrete activity to pass through pure thought."

The excellent praises of M. Fernandez, indeed, who saw Meredith freshly from his French distance, recall in their taut exaltation the fervours of our discovering youth and give pretext for their recollection.

Our own " exquisite reasons " could never compare with his excellent fine-spinning. If we are not philosophical critics besides, it matters less to us that Meredith "beheaded romanticism." But the philosophical interpretations of M. Fernandez, though couched in subtleties which a Meredith could understand better than most of us, though modernly wrapped up in all the modern sanctions of the modern spirit, seem to say pretty much the kind of thing we used to say in our old-fashioned and obvious superlatives: concerning that " astounding precursor who," says M. Fernandez, "was writing in the days of George Eliot novels which still seem to us today audacious and oriented toward the future." And M. Fernandez's initial choice of theme was made, as was our own long ago, not primarily for love of art but for love of life: " Is not this the time to set about knowing the writer who, thanks to his exceptional organization, had the privilege alone among his fellows of bequeathing to us the magnificent heritage of hope? "

The heritage of hope, yes, say we who have long known him, because the heritage of health. Our second thoughts are sure to concern themselves with experiments of art and such proprieties. But the first grip of Meredith came not indeed from his consistent adherence to his favourite principles of comedy nor from the flashes of his unequal poetic imagination. Rather is his work in prose and verse felt first to be a monument to sanity in human life. The body of his novels is wide in scope, sounding the scale of experi-

ence from pure lightness of heart to the depths where
"the worst returns to laughter." But the maudlin
moment is never ratified, nor the whimper of self-
pity, nor the solitary complaint against an unfeeling
universe. Here is sanity uncompromising and imperturbable. There is tonic in the energy, healing in the
ruthlessness. For the world-weary Empedocles, type
of all loose-gripped humanity, there is but the terse
epitaph:

> "He jumped. With none to hinder,
>   Of Aetna's fiery scoriae
>   In the next vomit-shower made he
>   A more peculiar cinder."

So perish all his despairing sort, unhelped by George
Meredith unless they are wise to find in exposure of
their bravado a sufficient help.

II

It was indeed as the priest of sanity that Meredith
chose to call himself comedian and captured for himself the word. We feel obliged to mention him when
we use it. For to Meredith, we are in the habit of
saying, more than to any other except his favourite
Molière, comedy means but the perfect exercise of
the intellectual faculty, busied with the honesty and
shapeliness of men, devoted to the stripping of folly
self-deceived. Like the comic spirit, the comic novelist must aim at unblinking penetration, to set in the
light the secret and unsuspected sin. Like the comic

spirit too, he must view his subject from sufficient distance if he would perceive it in its right proportions, would keep the freedom from prejudice which may purge away contempt, " a sentiment which cannot be entertained by comic intelligence." *The Egoist* is a plainer statement of the creed than the *Essay on Comedy*. And in *Beauchamp's Career* is voiced most deliberately the novelist's artistic aim: " This day, this life, and even politics, the centre and throbbing heart of it, must be treated of, men and the ideas of men, — these are my theme; and may it be my fortune to keep them at blood-heat and myself calm as a statue of Memnon in prostrate Egypt. He sits there, waiting for the sun, — I here, and readier to be musical than you think. I can at any rate be impartial. And do but fix your eyes on the sunlight striking him, and you have an idea of the passive receptivity of sun and shade that I hold it good to aim at if at the same time I can keep my characters at blood-heat." So ever and anon in the various appeals of his poetry he stops to glorify the comic genius, the "sword of common sense," hence the sword of the spirit without which we none of us shall see salvation.

Comedy then may be at once a religion and the condition of sound art. It is the worship of naked sincerity and moral health; it tries at the same time to create an atmosphere man-made where the vapours of morbidness are blown away and the oxygen of common sense is provided for the breathing. It is good air for the realist who would talk his old talk in new language. It is good air, when the chemical achievement is really achieved, for all literary energies.

Thus the course of Meredith's fiction was one long contribution to the human intelligence which was his light; and to bear witness to that light came into existence the various and complex characters which he created in the chambers of his imagery. All the better is their testimony that in most cases they have failed in the ordeal, for with one exception the novels of Meredith centre about some poor tragic-comedian "who has struck a discord with life," gone somehow trippingly astray in the path of "unreason and sentimentalism," "such being Folly's parentage when it is respectable." We know them all — the seekers after delicate affectation, the victims of blind self-delusion, the blind who boast of sight, the feeble who pretend to strength, a considerable train of lovable unconscious fools who have sought all in some unsuspected manner after vanity.

There is the warm and erratic beauty of Diana, hasty-footed, quick to folly, wilful for a bullet's shot at a swiftly sighted aim. There are the sentimentalists of *Sandra Belloni*, with whom Meredith almost forgets his boasted patience: the delicately ludicrous Poles, twittering group of triflers who turn to prettiness their loves, their hopes, and the deepest experiences of life. There are the self-deluding charlatans: the stupendous fraudulence of Richmond Roy, the presumptions of Old Mel's children and their victim, the delightful Evan, struggling through the network of deceit in which he is so carefully entangled to honesty's freedom. There are the pitiful self-deceivers, who fail only through an overweening sense of their own importance. Poor Sir Austin Feverel, in the vain attempt to be Providence to his son, apes too much the aloofness of Providence, learning too late the mercy of Providence. More gallant is the failure of our favourite Beauchamp, sweet and noble of nature, failing in humility only from the intensity of his conviction which drives him headlong to bring to pass at once the deed upon the thought: "His mind was clear enough to put the case that either he beheld a tremendous magnification of things or else that other people did not attach common importance to them, and he decided that the latter was the fact." Alas for Beauchamp! But in reverence before his inglorious end we learn respect as nowhere else even in the pages of Meredith for the modesty of human reason.

Comedy which is effectively relentless must concern itself with plot. The comic conception of human nature is intrinsically dramatic, demanding continuous and inexorable logic of action, a steadily thickening web woven by the victim himself. It is no longer necessary to take sides in the old argument as to whether *The Egoist* is a masterpiece or a disgrace in plot construction. To busy oneself overmuch today with criticism of plot-technique is to be as out-moded as is Huxley in his preoccupation with Gadarene swine. But at least the Meredithian story is rich with a plurality of complications, unified by a reach of vision which perceives the end toward which the

varied and branching courses of folly must ultimately
stream, with extraordinary and inevitable results of
stripping and discomfiture. *The Egoist* with all its
bewildering variety is of course the simplest exponent
of the author's method. The very sound of Sir Willoughby's name conjures up the image of his correct
figure and well-moulded face so perfect that the
slightest surprise precipitates it into caricature. Re-
gardful for the dignity of his own being, he balances
gracefully on the base of his egotism till the due
tumble exposes him to his abhorrence, " the world."
As we watch his shifts to escape ridicule, we let no
pity mitigate our judgment but join the sprites of
laughter who circle perpetually about the figure of
Sir Willoughby to celebrate a victim so peculiarly to
their liking. A man acts according to the folly of his
nature, and there is a multifarious plot; its revelation
is a dramatic climax.

Meredith had the wisdom to put his " sun " beside
his " shadow." We do not forget that the maker of
Beauchamp and Willoughby made also those creations of full-blooded vigor, potent with sincerity and
unerring truth, who come and go through the meshes
of the woven story. Theirs is the gift to find out the
way of nature in the doubtful paths of folly and of
ruin vapor-wrought, for they pass in a grace of
moral health able to cure and to revive. We know
them best among George Meredith's making, for
they are his immortal women, dearest types of unqualified genuineness. Into the network of her children's lies walks the inexorable Mrs. Mel, bent on

the rescue of Evan to rational life. If Sir Austin Feverel would have consulted Mrs. Berry, plump incorporation of the sure maternal instinct, she could have given him an aphorism better than any of his, " that it's al'ays the plan in a dielemmer to pray God and walk forward." There is the fidelity of the French René, the staunch devotion of English Janet, the charm of Clara Middleton, fairest of the lovely women of George Meredith. And unconscious among the " fine shades " and the " nice feelings " moves Sandra Belloni in her simplicity, as lonely amid their unreality as the sound of her glorious voice in the silence of the night-empty woods, appeal to whatsoever within us is genuine and straightforward.

Thus Meredith's work exceeded his aim; for the true believers must refuse to accept his limitation as comedian. Of wit he sufficiently convinced us long ago — it has become a popular argument against him. There is more need to emphasize that illumined sympathy which can probe unreason without trace of malignity, which can turn dissection of folly to a scene of beauty. Even too much has been said of the idyllic light which rests upon the loves of Richard and Lucy Feverel. None may smile except in gentleness at the meeting by the river, the poetry of the wood-talk under the moon, while boor, scoffer, and sentimentalist listen in the bushes; or at the tale of Richard's wandering in the wet woods, tremulous over the birth of his child. From the same mind came the baleful tragedy of *Rhoda Fleming,* record of anguish miserably needless, crushed to silence. Hence came too that other tragedy of *Vittoria* where the comic faculty, slumbering for once, leaves us sober but alert before the dignity of mortal pain, free to pass beyond the personal problem to the historic significance of events in a world of space and action, aglow with contest, big with event, swept by time.

The faults of Meredith are never faults of dullness. An unlimited zest for plot entanglement must sometimes result in a woof too elaborate for unnimble wits or for good control. He who has for a lifetime conceived his characters by a systematic exercise of the comic perception must sometimes fail of reality, reduce his handiwork to the precision of a mechanism. Often enough we are rebuffed by insistence on the critical attitude, by a theory pushed beyond the human limit. Yes, there are long chapters and long books indeed — and their number increases by exposure to time — when the dynamo revolves with wasteful magnificence. There is coldness in our hearts at sight of Lord Fleetwood's meteoric vagaries, Lord Ormont's wanton tempting of joy, or the shallowness of Victor Radnor's optimism. But for this once we did not choose to harp upon lapses in work so various, so thoughtful, so complex. Complexity indeed, in the old-fashioned sense of the word, is our final impression of Meredith's fiction.

III

It is always with some surprise that we perceive the real simplicity at the heart of his poetry. We can

recognize our novelist in the kindly monologues like
" Juggling Jerry," in the tragic force of " Modern
Love," in the subtle pride of Theodolinda's high fervour. But the dearest aim — to make picture-writing,
is clearly won. It is picture-writing both exact and
lordly, winged with colour, kingly flashing, rich with
moving gold, blown in on the light in a world which
dips before the breeze. It writes good promise too;
for in his poetry Meredith gives full utterance to his
buoyancy, to his whole-hearted acceptance of life's
secret.

For Meredith's faith resolves itself at last to the
mere sensation of Nature's beneficence, the persuasion that to follow the law of earth is the way of
blessing. His truest type of man is the giant Antaeus,
whose strength returns at every touch of the ground.
Even the poetry of Meredith's age breathes assurance: that struggle is progress, that change is the
way of beauty's new birth, that the base of sky-
climbing hope is in dirt-soil. Turn to the titles of the
collected volumes; and, whether it be the *Reading of
Earth* or the *Reading of Life*, the meaning is always
the *Joy of Earth*.

To such wisdom, then, whether or not it can sen-
sibly be called philosophy, Meredith calls back the
children of men as to the only sanity. It is wholesome wisdom, and that it comes not of reasoning but
of mystic reverence is its saving grace for poetry. It
is warm with the wonder of created things, with the
bliss of growth, with man's inner kinship for whatever lives on the face of the earth. Thus the symbolic

poem, " The Woods of Westermain," which typifies
most profoundly the poet's trust in nature's kindliness to him who loves her fully, bids us "foot at
peace with mouse and mole," "love the light so
well " as to fear no darkness. Then and then only do
we catch "the clue of earth"; then only do we gain
the " fruitful sight" and escape the dire revelation
of earth's terrors which awaits inexorably the con-
sternation of the doubter. A mystic creed! None the
worse a creed for that, a tranquil creed which makes
no assault upon the ineffables, nor asks:

> " The silent to give sound,
> The hidden to unmask,
> The distant to draw near."

In this earth-worship, despite his "tumbling
verses" and his unclassical luxuriance, Meredith
approaches the spirit of the Greeks. Not for all their
divinities has he honour — never indeed for Dio-
nysus, leader in life's madness, little perhaps for the
goat-foot Pan, " a holiness horn and heel "; but he
turns with comprehension to the light-giver Apollo,
maker of songs "whose harmonies all are sane," and
with best sympathy to the great mother Demeter,
type of earth's renewing, who brings the joy of
abundance. His masterpiece is probably " The Day
of the Daughter of Hades," story of the maid who
escaped from the pale land of the dead for one day
of light and the knowledge of things that grow. If a
myth might be conscious of its own beauty, here were
a made myth at last, full-measured with the fatness

of earth, the wonder of life's milky kernel, " corn,
wine, fruit, oil," a song which " gives us to eat." For
the shadow-born could sing as no mortal of the
" rapture of breath," " the grace of the battle for
food." The poem will find a place, we may hope,
among the permanent things, — fair with world's
beauty and bloom, fairer in its reverence for earth's
yield of increase, for the mellow fruitfulness of harvest. Here more perfectly than in his profounder
works is underlying peace sun-lightened. It is an old
wisdom which our lean years can hardly recall. But
it is wisdom as the under-hum of poetry's song. Here
from the midst of small singing, sighers after forgotten things, yearners at beauty's passage, came a
strong field note, strong for the piping of years, in
hard weather and in blossom-season, a paean of the
joy of earth.

With the pictorial qualities of verse to help we
best understand and best forgive Meredith's obscurity in style. For it is not, we perceive, obscurity
of affectation, nor obscurity of vagary, but of fresh
language freshly cut. In the poetry, where it is less
frequent, it is obscurity of failure, unhappy part of
defective technique — for we must frankly acknowledge a host of inequalities and breaks in tone, of
shocks in taste, of intrusive *bizarrerie,* of offences
against lyricism and poetic dignities. The jungle of
speech has been too thick for the pioneering knife.
But the obvious labour in sweat of the brow is sufficiently disarming to our complaint. Disarming too
are some clear simplicities of the finished word, —

so fine is the picture-writing, so bold and sound the achieved clarity of the nature verses.

The prose, too, is fresh-cut though by no means helpless. For Meredith has not written, we must protest, as the conceited jackanapes, even on the loudest days of the rumbling dynamo. He has written only as the Englishman of bold and wilful prose tradition, held provincial by Arnold and his ilk, — taking his liberties, respecting his caprice, saying his individual say in his individual terms without the slightest pains to be understood. He has loved to play cunningly with words and thoughts and dictates the game to his readers, to baffle by a deliberate habit of rapid change, by a jumbling of many styles assumed without notification, by a sudden slip from nonsense to tragic simplicity, from epigram to volubility. Always we must reckon with his habit of abridged expression, a descriptive stenography so direct at its best as to mystify by force. Always we must reckon with his unannounced analogies quick with so diverse suggestion that the reader accustomed to a slacker vocabulary misses meaning a-quiver with reality, so straight its rush at the target. The fault is simply the wrong side of Meredith's gift, — that knack for accurate thought and accurate speech which, touched with wonder, achieves poetry or, graced with wit, is the extreme condensation of sense.

For Meredith's work may be likened by the true believer to the very tree of knowledge which according to the old narrative of Cyrano de Bergerac, grows in the garden of the moon: " Its fruit is covered with a rind which produces ignorance in whomsoever hath tasted thereof; yet this rind preserves underneath its thickness all the spiritual virtues of this learned food." So is it with Meredith's fruitage. The bite is hard for the tooth; but within the finest specimens is a learned food indeed, tasting of nothing less than the knowledge of good and evil.

II

T. E. BROWN

I

THE query — Does not God walk in gardens? —
is almost the only bit of T. E. Brown's often
delightful poetry well known to the present revised
generation. Brown had the luck to write on two subjects with which contemporary *belles lettres* are but
slightly occupied, the Isle of Man and religion. The
Isle of Man, as outpost of Celtic consciousness, has
fulfilled the dark foreboding of its poet and become
a place very like another. And who so bold as to
publish an essay on somebody's religious poetry unless, as in the present case, the theme be carefully
postponed until the end? The mediaeval inquiry:

" Spyrytualete! What the devyll may that be? "
sounds more natural today than it can have sounded
in its own time. But gardens have never quite gone
out of style since Eden. And many a garden-lover,
though he may be otherwise heathenish enough, is
still willing in good weather to endorse the pleasant
confession of faith:

" Not God? In gardens! When the day is cool?
  Nay, but I've a sign.
'Tis very sure he walks in mine."

Yet it is to be feared that even the gentle gardener has made but few inquiries about T. E. B.

Brown at least would never hold us excused, blessed as he was with a knack for literary pieties and instructed admirations. "Fancy," he writes, "going into the presence of your Maker and having to admit that you have never read *The Fortunes of Nigel*." His own claims were more modest. He would never have seriously placed his minor abundance beside the larger plenties. But he would feel some surprise unpickled by corrosive vanity to conceive a generation of readers all unaware of *Fo'c's'le Yarns* or of that "rum 'un," Tom Baynes, admiral of story-tellers before the mast. We have seized the hackneyed excuse for critical house-cleaning: 1930 was the centenary of Brown's birth. But the work of T. E. B. is no attic stuff, no vesture to be folded up. His spirit is a veritable though innocent *diable boiteux*, too buoyant ever to have deserved a corking. To release it even to oneself is to catch in the face a tonic breath, an escape of sun and air.

Perhaps the trouble has been that Brown wrote too much. All too few, indeed, are his personal poems, published in the last volume, *Old John and other Poems*, of which the best seem to have been written between 1868 and 1878. Scanty, too, and undeservedly neglected in files of the Henley periodicals are his essays, recollections of Oxford's days and dons and of literary excitements, on themes as variant as Pusey and Izaak Walton, sprinkled with beautiful bits of that uncommon thing, beautiful English prose. But the main body of his work, the long monologues in Anglo-Manx, though delightful in a frank old-fashioned way, is even appallingly extensive.

T. E. B. too has been but moderately committed to the perpetual care of biography. But his letters, collected in 1903, though clipped by many an editorial reserve and limited by the omission of many years, are a capital substitute. They show with a sort of triumphant survival the man as his friends knew him — a man essentially manly and simply good; rugged as the child of Manx rigour and poverty should be, strong and stern in control, sustained in reticence but warm at heart from elemental fires, headlong and complete in generosities, unfailing in friendship, magnificent in mimicry, stoical in quietude, splendid in wit.

They reveal, besides, the curiously duplex character of his life and work. They show him obviously as he wished to be, the master-Manxman, scholar-poet of the folk. They show him with more reticence but more profoundly, the "born solitary," the contemplative in the midst of fellowship and business, whose utterance was the religious lyric, remote in its nature and appeal from the homely warmth of the dialect yarnings.

They suggest, too, all the facts that we need to know. They recall the birth in the cottage parsonage near Douglas of the young one among the many children of a poor clergyman, to a life "carepricked" yet "healed with balm of sea and rock."

They note the struggle for education at last ended, the distinguished degree which made the young servitor of Christ Church actually first among Oxford's youth, the fellowship at Oriel in Oriel's greatest day. They touch lightly on the farewell to academic vegetarianism, the choice of marriage and the common tug. They complain with humorous frankness at the schoolmaster's career, that pill accepted though never quite digested, even through the thirty years as second master of Clifton. A stanza of 1869 records the always slumbering protest:

" I'm here at Clifton, grinding at the mill
    My feet for thrice nine barren years have trod;
But there are rocks and waves at Scarlet still,
    And gorse runs riot in Glen Chass —
            thank God! "

For the most part the letters tell of the last four years, the return to the Isle of Man, which was resolved upon almost by accident at a visit's end, the flight of the homing-bird back to the "blaeberries on old Barrule" and the "silence still on Carragh." They reveal an always closer dedication to what the writer called "Islandhood."

"Absolutely and really I could live here forever with a Horace," he writes. The quotation suggests the special compound of learning and power of unlearning which was one secret of Brown's difference from others. There was understanding of things elementary and bare, so necessary that he felt himself elsewhere a starveling. " I did very well in the Isle of

Man," he writes after one visit, "had two solitary walks, drank deep draughts of I don't know how to describe it — that social brewage which is got nowhere else." But the Horace was necessary, almost a symbol of his intellectual life fed on the honeydew of scholarship, symbol besides of the nice preparation which he believed necessary for whoso would undertake to interpret the rough. So he trained himself to be a dialect-poet on a fare of Virgil and Euripides, with an almost Chinese dedication to the rites of memory, shedding tears (of another sort from the usual schoolboy's) at thought of what the *Ars Poetica* had been to him. His classical faith he confessed with a mingling of his own paradox and a sort of Athanasian flair: " Greek is a baptism into a faith, a cult, not more irrational than other faiths and cults, the baptism of a regeneration which releases from I know not what original sin; and if a man does not see that, he is a fool, and such a fool that I shouldn't wonder if he gravely asked me to explain what I mean by original sin in such connection." " I know whom I have believed," he says elsewhere of Virgil. It is a late and nice word of classicism, this seagrowth by the Manx strand. But not Euripides nor Horace nor Virgil is stellified in Brown's heaven. Each is brought in turn to be most winningly " the genius of the shore," friendly as any Manxman of them all.

The letters are foaming with expressiveness. A gallant phrase is always to Brown like a good drink or a whiff of mountain air. "After all," he says somewhere, "I don't mind confessing that I have many times constructed a whole system of little more than bosh to enshrine a 'locution.' Faith, one might do worse." But Brown is not among those to whom bosh should ever be forgiven, so fresh is his power over speech, so self-driven his thought. Here is prose at once ingenuous and precious. And the word prose meant in Brown's vocabulary no second best. "It is true," he wrote to a friend, "that at your time of life the poetic mustum might well have been raked off and the pure and limpid prose be beautifully on tap, ready for drinking."

One could perhaps get a considerable raking of mustum from Brown's own verse, but never from his letters. Each is, in a way, like his characteristic poem, a dramatic monologue, setting in like a breeze, not assumed like a garment, through which drift keen ardours, wit fair and familiar, eruditions sun-warmed and floating free. One remembers another Thomas Browne, liked and once plundered by this namesake — in the savours and flavours, the privacies of invention, especially in the liberty taken with the Latin word, though Sir Thomas Browne would never have dreamed of such impudence. But the verbal audacities are niceties of abandon which the classics could never resent, being so sweetly entreated. We understand the old charge of self-consciousness brought against T. E. B. But it is like the play of his little mountain brook just beginning its infant wiles in the water still spring-cold:

"O brave leap! brave leap!
'Twas excellently done!

. . . .

Have at the biggest stone — O nobly meant!
I swear it was magnificent! . . ."

So do the cherubs show off, it is to be hoped, in the kingdom of heaven.

The same gusto is everywhere for all things sound. Most delicately it waited on a flower. It watched the transubstantiation of the elements in the miracles of mountain light. It was always ready for a mountain climb twenty miles long and arduous all the way. It was ready for all generous admirations: for master spirits or at least manly spirits discerned in the world of letters, for just men made lately perfect, or for living and familiar friends:

"'Croak — croak — croak!
Do you like your own folk?'
'Yes,' says the little Jackdaw."

It was ready till the last day for every whiff of air that came from the Isle of Man.

The Isle of Man, "far withdrawn into the golden west," became by habit and deliberation his sufficient life,

"A little island in the sea,
A body for my needs."

His affection could perceive its poverty: "You can hardly believe," he writes in an early letter, "how absolutely barren and desolate the island appears to me coming from Gloucestershire." But once made, the confession is never repeated. All his "dreaming" is charged with the vision of "island forms," with the search of austere winds, "the cliff, the beach, the tide, the rock," "where salt winds whistle through the bent," with the roughness of sea-holly under foot, with the sad "cluck of water in the tangles," with the mist of open spaces, and at dusk:

> "that strange drift-light, dim, forlorn,
> Of the sun's wreck and clashing surges born."

Brown's best days were on sunny upland slopes in the regions of cleanest air, where the heather "rushes," where the gorse bloom "bubbles." The step always springs upward — not indeed to walk in sentimental mood with morning on the silver horns, but maybe to sit naked on a rock below the waterfall in the eyes of silly sheep, alone as a god, or in sheer vitality to pose upon a watershed "as upon a horse" — "up with the blessed mosses, and the sweet golden gurgle" of the little singing streams "that have been saying the same things since dry land appeared." In the grim whimsy of "Dartmoor" the celestial surgeon comments on a vivisection of the poet's brain:

> "Another lancet — thanks!
> That's Manx, —
> Yes, the delicate, pale, sea-green
> Passing into ultra-marine —
> A little blurred — in fact
> This brain seems packed
> With sunsets."

With the years the exalted celebration of nature yielded to the deeper, half-conscious fellowship. He confessed to something of the limpet in his make-up. "Solidarity with this globe, daedal or non-daedal, makes me happy enough." More and more the doings of sophisticated man became an inconsiderable triviality in comparison with "this largeness — A whole bench of bishops throned on South Barrule! What would it add?"

Yet most deeply rooted in Brown was the sense of human tradition, the continuity of the generations. "One thing often touches me," he writes, "the deserted villages which are the result of emigration — the cold hearth, the bit of thorn where children have played, the elder-tree at the gable to keep away the fairies. And the vacant space, just so many feet of vacant air — the home, the place where the bed was, where babies have been born and women wept." His filial piety was deeply solemn with an outspoken frankness which was certainly not due to the Saxon within him — for his father, the sainted "persoun of a toun," for the mother of Borderer stock from whom he drew his strength and mountain love. Always the quality of race made for him the best romance. At a feast of Burns he became "fairly mad with seempathy": "Heaven only knows what crapula inherited from generations of toddy-drinking Borderers takes possession of me."

Brown's family tree had but very little "Celtic root in the Isle of Man," though he liked to think of himself as wholly Manx. But he made the most of the Celt within him, a good deal hardened, as he felt, by Saxon qualifications. He used the thought, as it were, to warm his hands. In his most glorious hours he is like another whom he describes as " dripping all over with Celtic rapture, like a dog just emerged from a pool and shaking himself." In quieter moments he dreams the Celtic dreams with deliberate choice. And of all imaginable bonds of kinship and race he makes religion: " The thought that troubled me was this — Who is to perpetuate the traditions? They must go with me. The whole business will be only a blank, not only tribal traditions but family. . . . The wind passeth over it and it is gone and the place thereof knoweth it no more. The new generation must build the fibre of its own and the old must vanish. I alone have to build a cairn of memories in my books."

II

His care, then, was only to be the poet of Manxland, to " hold the mirror up to his countrymen." The *Fo'c's'le Yarns* are dedicated to this aim. They are " soaked in dialect," " colloquial," in the language, we are to believe, of the forecastle, or of the mine and beach, " with the thundering verbs, the outrageous adjectives one hears at the Harbour," with vocabulary further enlarged, we naturally suppose, by the invention of that most expressive Manxman, Brown himself. The poems, long and bulky, are meant " to unlock the Island heart," to " secure

an anchor for the Celtic soul," if ever future men
of the Isle start " haply longing for their fathers."
Brown laboured indefatigably, and largely in vain,
for a Manx revival, lecturing on Island themes,
hoarding every scrap of the apparently unremark-
able Manx verse, welcoming any attempts such as
Hall Caine's to make Man a serious basis for novel
or poem, concocting Island songs with no vanity
about their value. For the Island's sake he poured
out his best years, refusing toward the end to accept
the archdeanery of the place, resolved to end a loyal
Manx life in free fellowship and literary service of
the Manx folk. For the Island's sake he mourned,
though quietly, in his last year, " the drying up of
the spring."

His personal ambition was sunk in wistful hope
for the awakening of the Island genius. In a letter
of good nonsense he once conceived the Manx poet
yet to be in whose glory he was content to be
eclipsed. " It is odd," he says of his own poems,
" but, do you know, I have a perfectly serene confidence in their future. How it will come about I am
unprepared to say, nor does it matter. A great poet
is yet to be, a Manx poet, transcending all our smaller
doin's. A child perhaps yet unborn will do it. He will
be called Kewish, Shimin, Quayle, Cottier — all
right. He will stumble across my old ditties. He
will love them. . . . The fire will be kindled. . . .
Through Kewish I shall find utterance, through
Quayle, through Cottier. . . . And I shall be perfectly satisfied. Kewish shall shed the tear of sym-

pathetic divination. Leave it to Kewish. A gran'
chap, Kewish."

Alas, no Kewish has arisen to fulfil this advent
prophecy, nor do we look any longer for his coming.
The partial critic may doubt, perhaps, whether such
a Kewish is deserved by a world which has mislaid
and in a sort forgotten *Fo'c's'le Yarns,* though the
late proud recollection of Brown on his hundredth
birthday may mean that the Isle of Man has found
in him its sufficient Kewish.

Interpretation of the Manx character in the letters is like clear-weather sunshine which sets everything off at its best. Its idealism is amusing in
contrast with the unglamorous recollections of down-
right brother Hugh Stowell Brown, the famous
Liverpool preacher, who recalled a folk without
grace, conditioned by drink and dirt, living in damp
cottages by an unkempt shore. Within the sentinel
cliffs, as T. E. B. saw them, lay a pure strand washed
by perpetual lustration; and the race which dwelt
thereby was "a darling race" still preserving a
primitive quality not yet denatured: "The Manx
life that is unrelated to England I find to be deeper,
stronger, richer, than I had thought, driven in upon
itself and curiously coloured by the fact." The folk
have "a spring of friendliness, throwing themselves
upon you with warmth and fun and vigour of talk
and accent." In the best he finds "a boundless curiosity, the thirst for knowledge miscellaneous, pulpy,
and piquant, which characterizes those who dwell
remote." In moments of despondency he admits

faults, such as a habit of irresponsible assertion: "The whole island seems strewn with rubbish of slatternly overstatement. It would be quite refreshing to take a walk in the narrowest and least decorated lane of simple truth." But for the most part the Island mind is neither dull nor untrue, but agog for marvel: "They look dismally at you if you enclose the smallest atom of space from the great common of the unexplained. Quite at home in the primordial embrace, they snuggle to it and are happy." They have "a length of reflection, a hilarity with which they range the far horizons of thought." They have unconscious reach into the depths, like divers: "There is a surface sparkle of chatter, and then with an 'Aw bless my soul,' or an 'Ay, man, ay,' they are down into the deepest soundings of the spirit." Such people were still assuredly known to Brown, living in this place apart, "without these nations and their noise."

The verses of Manxland are all stories. These made the "protoplasm enough for poetry" which Brown always found on every return to the Island. "I believe," he wrote on a holiday from Clifton, "that if I were living here permanently, I should get a whole cart-load of this lore. I had no idea that such a number of silk-worms were here, spinning their quaint cocoons night and day. The brains are always going. I almost heard them at it. I didn't sleep all through the nights." Brown's editors tell us that the actual body of his poems was all composed before he made the Island his permanent

home. But the gleanings from the fleeting visits
make a sufficient pack. The themes seem much the
same on the Isle of Man as elsewhere: " courtesy,
humanity, friendliness, hardiness, love, friendship,
murder, hate, virtue, and sin." There have been no
new stories since King Arthur's day.

Shorter dialect poems reveal often the minor
humours. Travellers in a stage are disconcerted to
find that they have been riding in a new Noah's ark
with " a lil cauf, ma'am " and " jus' a lil donkey."
In happy vein a bluff sailor father returns from his
cruise just in time for the christening of the son he
has never seen, and remembers that on the very
birth-day he saw

> " a baby as plain
> Passin' by on a slant of rain."

But the tale of pity is more recurrent than the jest,
especially the pitifulness of maternity and the sorrows forever multiplied upon it. Most praised of
Brown's poems is the poignant " Mater Dolorosa "
in which a mother, still dazed by the death of a nursing child, comforts the husband who " cusses " in
grief, by notions of an angelic heaven with a friendly
Jesus who would probably take an occasional look
at all babies, though in her heart she still doubts
the tenderness of celestial nursing:

" Will they take him up when he's wanting takin' ? "

The best tales, in themselves a wide representa-
tion of Manx life, are the *Fo'c's'le Yarns* told by

Quartermaster Tom Baynes to a forecastle audience held and in a sort compelled by the masterly spinning — of scenes as they used to be back home at the Harbour, in the fishing-boats, among the miners, on the remote farms in the pockets of the hills, in the villages packed with closer life. The local events are all here: the fairing and its turbulence, the harvest home, the storm, the shipwreck, the drowning, the gallant rescue, the visitation of cholera still terrible in memory, the coming of the " Ranters " and the excitements of religious conversion, the discovery of a Chartist refugee in " hilding," and, sad and frequent theme, the betrayal of woman, the return of the prostitute to be sternly deported by the inexorable judgment of the folk — rivalries between town and mine, between shore and upland, and a perpetual courting expressively called " sooreying." Broken hearts are perhaps too frequent; for of the young girls " hapes of them, lovely as light," some have died of love from time to time, it seems, in the Isle of Man.

The *Yarns* have a lively population of real Manx folk liked with the enthusiasms of the letters but known at their worst as well as at their best, just as we know the neighbours. They are for the most part inexpressive, with one idea and that a simple one at a time, tormented by no subtleties but bewildered often by themselves, driven hard by impulses beyond their ken. They are compound of passions low-moving on the level of the beast or exalted in purity. They are children boisterous and

rough, for whom none the less a burst of poetry or
of beauty may happen any time. They are casting
nets in the sea, delving deep in the soil, stupendous
in drunkenness, gripped by tradition including the
longest tradition of dirt. Sturdy housewives gossip
in doorways or make stupid malice in parlours;
children are thick underfoot. Real hearts alive
tramp through the muddy streets. And above all is
Tom Baynes.

Tom Baynes, the special creation of T. E. B., is
surely not made to be forgotten. He is master story-
teller, a " dreamer " in his own sense of the word:

" A dream, it's like — and it's strange to a man,
But I'm allis seein' things that's gane."

He is the Manx character of Brown's day, as he con-
ceives it at its simple best, in its uncouthness and its
wisdom — Manx with genius added. In his utterance a word comes always heightened, colloquialized,
dramatized. Take a bit of transformation on a familiar theme:

" But I'm allis thinkin' of the fellow once —
In the Bible, you know — that said to his brother,
' Pull out the moat! ' ' Indeed,' says the other;
' Is it moats? ' he says; ' And talkin' to me!
Come out o' that with that beam! ' says he."

The tales are bulky; for the teller likes each one
and is minded to make the most of his opportunity.
They are long not only because finespun but because
they wander both unconsciously and with resolution,

pausing without excuse to elaborate a picture, a flavour, a memory, a sorrow. The audience waits, impatient, while Tom falls into a reverie, uniting in his vision and ours the forecastle audience and the faraway recollections of youth and home. But most in these lapses Tom shows himself poet in his gift of " knawin'."

" Noticin' lek! " " Semperthisin'! " " Takin' a terr'ble interer'! " Such is the way of Tom Baynes. He is alive — to the feeling of things, to the " spring of an innocent foot," to the wind that "blows straight from the farm," to the milk "tearin' into the can," to the mystery and motion of the world's processes:

" Like the moon and the stars God only touched,
    Once long ago and away they scutched;
    And now He never minds them a bit,
    But they keep goin' on, for they're used of it."

His best " knawin' " is for the devious ways of human nature, its evasions and subterfuges, more revealing than its central acts. He reads the lines of experience on the worn faces, as in the moment when he tells his mother that he is off to sea:

" And I looked in her face, and the shape and strent,
    And the very face itself had went
    All into one like a sudden thaw,
    Slished and slushed, or the way you've saw
    The water bubblin' and swirlin' around
    The place where a strong man have gone down."

He has an aphoristic sense which a Meredith might respect: the wisdom of the folk plus a shrewdness of his own:

" Pardonin'? Murderers? What do they want?
  God can afford it, but man can't."

    ". . . When a bone
Is picked, it's better to lave it alone."

" And never no egg wasn't hatched with bilin'."

" This is love! " she said, " and the nice it would be
  If it wasn' for the misery! "

Brown identified himself with Tom Baynes as he wrote. " I never stopped for a moment to think what Tom Baynes should be like. He simply *is* I." Brown's assertion should not be taken literally. Tom Baynes is but a rough diamond. He defends the accepted doctrines of Christianity by the direct method of throwing a budding atheist off the coach. His special pride is a fine art of spitting which he teaches his initiates. But the resemblance is evident and amusing. One remembers the report that mimicry in conversation was almost a second nature to Brown. He must have put on the sailor's cap and tattoo without noticing. One discerns the Tom Baynes manner even in a late essay on Sir Philip Sidney. And perhaps Tom Baynes is actually responsible for our recent loss of memory about him.

Brown is far too easy-going in his ways, though his laxity is no more than the " fine, eupeptic slovenliness " which he has liked in another — " sheer garrulity, affectionate, of course, nice and cosy, but still garrulity." Tom Baynes, a " comf'ble " creature, can hardly be too irregular to please us. But the verses of Brown reveal many such lapses in places far less appropriate than the *Yarns*. It is often hard to descry the line which runs between whimsy and absurdity, and Brown does not always note on which side he is stepping. Is a daring phrase a bit of splendour or a lack of self-criticism? We are not surprised to hear Brown say that the verses sometimes went on in his sleep. Such ease is always unlucky. Poets, and present day poets perhaps more than Brown, can always profit by the wisdom of the old Protestant divine: " If the work be a good work it is work. Ye can make but work of it." Brown himself knew his weakness. In a late year he wrote with acumen and humility to a younger man of letters on their common admiration for the finish and shapeliness of a newly discovered French novel: " I quite see how natural it is for certain minds to energize in that way, but then I can't. And that is settled forever and probably was settled some fifty years ago."

Tom Baynes may have increased besides the poet's unashamed penchant for pathos already considerable enough. Our poet seems here most old-fashioned, like the young Mrs. Gaskell or the young Dickens at any age. But it is quite harmless, this pathos of a buoyant and singing spirit. Brown was frankly conscious of his taste for tears and jested

about it without apology. " Perhaps you think me a
ninny, but whoever wrote ' The Pleasures of Melancholy ' just hit my notion if he did it well." And
the *Fo'c's'le Yarns* are washed in a flood of pitifulness. Brown knew, none better, the value of artistic
reticence, the "noble avenues of reserve through
which a strong spirit withdraws itself," on guard
over its depths. The sterling climber, he says, " treads
the heights above the watershed of the facile and
the lacrymose." We must agree with him. To achieve
the pathos of " Betsy Lee " or of " Mater Dolorosa "
is to express real life and magnanimity. It is nevertheless to miss the rigour which is " to enter in at
the strait gate." Yet whoso has spent some hours
with Tom Baynes in the forecastle will leave with
thanks and with no churlish word of criticism.

III

In the poetry not Anglo-Manx but Brown's own,
lyrical, speculative, descriptive, religious, there is
perhaps a finer value and a more than minor originality, not only in the brave vagary of rhythm, the
free-ranging verse in the days before freedoms of
verse got themselves talked about.

Resemblances to better known poets are evident
enough, as is natural where reading and sympathy
went wide. Those who remember Brown almost
hesitate to list his enthusiasms, so catholic and liberal and apparently contradictory his tastes. Among
English poets Wordsworth was his declared choice;

and the affinity is evident enough — in his singular reverence, tested by familiarity, for common man and in his dependence for daily food on the fellowship of nature. He suggests, as often though probably by accident, the buoyant or anguished Clough, in the animal verve of some nature verses and in the gallant pitting of his spirit against the universal secret. Browning, who admired T. E. B., must have found good not only the skillful monologue and the speculation like in boldness though not in power to his own, but also the carving of fresh galleries through the hard quarries of speech, though it never happened to Brown to disembowel a volcano or to stir a subterranean fire. Still the quality of Brown remains his own.

" Noticin'," "takin' an interes'," " realizin' " — these are still Brown's gifts in his delicate personal verses. We have seen his vision for the lines of experience on hard Manx faces. It is as keen for other faces, as in the late " Roman Women," where pass in full-blooded procession the noble mate for Brutus, the strong mother of young Romans, and their sisters dissolute and voluptuous under the hard Italian light. For all things under the air the " knawin' " is also a heightening: for the summer smell of the foxgloves, those " innumerous celled revolvers " which —

" Shoot honey-tongued quintessence of July "

in the garden which we have remembered, or for the apotheosis of a mouldy schooner late " rat-riddled,"

" slime-slobbered," become under the benediction
of the west a spirit bound for morning.

Brown's reflective verse is extemporaneous in
form as the *Fo'c's'le Yarns*. He has left a considerable body of elegiac poetry, notably in memory
of his son Braddan, who died at the age of seven. Of
these " Aber Stations " is remarkable, a series of
seven sorrows through which the mourning spirit,
fleeing from April jubilee and platitudinous con-
dolence, climbs to the keen air of the upper slopes
to the waterfall of memory, to find there relief and
acquiescence even in " the transcendent rush " of
spring. It has a persistence of minor memories, a
play of the stricken fancy with the desolate symbolism of loss, which is acquaintance with grief.
Often here, as in the smaller lyrics on the same
theme, there is a poignancy like the best of Coventry
Patmore. And otherwhere in the midst of many too
facile verses comes a check in the poetry of pain
which gives for the instant the force of an epigram.

The mind of Brown stirs itself healthily about the
mysteries. With Wordsworth he hearkens to nature.
But he is a pupil of quick question with the readi-
ness to attack the unanswering and the unanswer-
able which has been native to keen minds since
Adam, becoming conscious of himself on creation
day, felt of his legs and arms and inquired of air
and tree and sky whence he came and why. It is to
Brown's credit that he does not always imagine the
same reply. The poems of pain and inquiry, such as
the arresting " Dartmoor," are charged, most often

with reproach. The cry against the apathy of Nature is fresh again: " The ages fall:

" Helpless from out the rigour of thine arm."

And the creative divinity within the cloud, " on Chaos drifting," wasteful, blind in favour, seems alien, uncertain, dumb, compared to the temporal activity of man, " shaping the definite self," " sifting the elements," " with determined letter and sweet articulate voice." But Brown withdraws at the end from the claims of man, his little meanings, distinct though they be, his "agues of desire" futile as " zigzag lightnings scrabbled on a cloud." The speculative poems are sure to enter the cosmic patience rather than to insist on revolt. Brown's real answer to experience is not a philosophy but a religion.

The early letters of the boy to his mother embarrass the reader of today by the frank and astounding piety. With the years Brown shared, as poems and letters show, the doubts and wrestles of his decade. One reads a greater economy of assertion, a greater humility. But the constant note is of freedom from interior hubbub. We may understand enough from a letter written in his last year, in which he cites the witness of saints as warrant of faith: " They have seen the king in his beauty. Give them credit for honesty, for intelligence, for sympathy with human wants, for absolute fairness, for burning love. . . . With tottering steps I have accompanied them. But that was years ago. Now I don't want to totter but to walk steadily. Therefore

I say unhesitatingly, I believe. I have encouraged the glimpses. . . . Must I always be breaking stones upon the road to heaven, examining every rung of Jacob's ladder? Well, no. I have other things to do."

One gift of the mystic at least is that very power of interior loneliness which Brown's friends record. " Few men are capable of such retirement," he wrote of himself. " It is an awfully large order," he said in 1890, " but we really need three lives, the life of pedagogic activity, the social life nicely arranged and kept in hand and never regarded as serious, and the intellectual and spiritual life." Thus to this neighbour and prince of conviviality our social life is but an accident, like the chance propinquity of horses which stand in adjacent stalls and sometimes hear each other whinny and munch. And in the religious verses the isolation of self becomes of course a contemplative isolation, the solitude of the private soul. So in a little poem " Salve," a spiritual cave-dweller receives with gladness and welcome the traveller who brings with him faggots for a fire and leaves in the morning with blessing:

" They have a cheerful warmth, those ashes of the stone."

Yet the traveller must pass on: " His morning is not thine."

Brown could rid himself of the leaden garment of self-consciousness, that " idiot cheer of self " which is his reading of our human limitation. The escape is not solely a religious experience, appar-

ently not a reward for penitential purging. It comes
in some degree from sheer comfortableness. In an
unsanctified poem of 1868, " The Lily-Pool," he
envies a big-eyed cow lazily enjoying the summer
warmth and the cool water, watching the mirror below, quite unconscious of her reflection:

> "So may I ever look upon the lily-pool,
> Nor ever in the slightest care
> Why I am there,
> Why upon land and sea
> Is ever stamped the inevitable me."

And Brown's power as spiritual poet is that he could
in transcendent seconds overlook the universal
image of the self. Self-conscious in delightful ways,
he nevertheless forgot sometimes the luggage of desire. The complete saint would hardly bother to be
a poet, it is true. Yet Pater was right that the saint
and the poet have more in common than either has
with the child of this world.

Brown's mystic lyric, therefore, is a free thing, a
play of delightful notions. Sometimes it recalls the
daring of Father Tabb. But the natural suggestion
is of the seventeenth century with its "sparkle of
similitude," its hide and seek of " divine wit," its
trail of fancies staid or fine, changing " as the old
Proteus did." We note promptly and with amusement that Brown studied and lectured zestfully
upon Quarles. But the " pious fancies " of Quarles
have rather the elasticity of good rubber than the
liberty of air where Brown met his casual sunbeams.
And when all is said, the symbols of Brown are his

own, old in shape sometimes but with the fresh tone of the child's invented word.

To his secular fancy, indeed, all things follow an amazing law of analogy to something else. Three maidens are seen, dark-robed, descending to the shore in silence, and straightway —

" It seemed to me a sacrament of some stern creed
unblessed."

The word sacrament is even too frequent. In the Brownish sense the sacraments are all about us, visible signs of invisible friskiness. The symbolism is engaging and unaffected — but a new way of " realizin'." We have seen what a cow in a pool can mean. We accept naturally a water-spaniel, soft and silky, in the sunset-sea off Bristol. Brown has a busy personifying friendship with " the spirits that wait on all high places " and with " all the lovely, cause-less, unclaimed things." He gives them his personal greeting and expects reply. So he flouts at his favourite black-bird tuning at the moon or flirts with a blossoming May-bough. And as the laureate of mountain-streams he chaffs all the little brook-fellows in the highlands. Yet his is not the hack-neyed fallacy, a tiresome spinning of fancies because a fancy is easier than an idea. Rather it is a lively persuasion of the pressure and significance of natural forms, their " keen contention to express a finite thought."

His dedicated poems, few but best, have there-fore their right word in " Disguises." The lyrics are, as it were, emblems of a Musician apt to play

heavenly music if the virginals of the soul are kept
ready — of an unseen Fellowship which will keep
tryst if anybody else will intend to keep it — of a
shell lying on the sand which the Sea's capacity
might brim to the full if it were but sufficiently empty
of its own little contents. This last is the theme of
Brown's lyric " Indwelling," complete in symbolism,
firm in shape:

" If thou couldst empty all thyself of self,
  Like to a shell dishabited,
  Then might He find thee on the ocean shelf
  And say, ' This is not dead,' —
  And fill thee with Himself instead.
  But thou are all replete with very *thou*,
  And hast such shrewd activity,
  That, when He comes, He says: ' This is enow
  Unto itself — 'Twere better let it be.
  It is so small and full, there is no room for Me.' "

It is the ring of a distant glad cry in each religious
lyric that calls us back when we are turning away
with the reflection that this is very much the sort
of thing we have heard before. It recalls the animal
gusto of the youthful letters, but it is more. Sometimes it is imperturbable and mature:

       " If youth be thine,
           Spare not to drink its wine;
         If youth be fled,
             Hold up
             The golden cup —
         God's grapes are always red."

Sometimes it has the artless reach of that fine cry,
" Land Ho! " wistful but with recurring assurance
like a far horn of promise:

> " You cannot see the land, my land,
> You cannot see, and yet the land is there.
> My land, my land, through murky air —
> I did not say 'twas close at hand — "

In reality or in mirage it shines from the verse with
the lure of the fairy worlds in the west where the
Celtic vision has seen the islands of the young: a
" land of purple mist," " under a star," only " a
loom of land " truly, yet visible to the spirit. It is
a land to be descried, one might say, borrowing a
phrase, only by true " innocence of vision."

The survival of that innocence in adult work
active with speculation, warm with experience, is
Brown's final singularity. It is the utterance of a
simplicity not to be found for seeking. Who shall
find simplicity? Easier far to enter the mother's
womb and be born again. But Brown did, without
doubt, drift sometimes into its light in his long and
wandering solitudes among the heights. Hence in
gleams of illumination we lose with him for a second
the memory of mortal strains and ineffectual passes.
There come small rushes of flight when we seem to
hear the flutter of little wings, as if we had run inadvertently through an invisible cloud of the Holy
Innocents escaped from a Sienese painting and out
for a holiday. From that company perhaps comes the
glad, almost inaudible, cry from far away.

Is there around the seat of the Holy Ghost an invisible game of the cherubic multitude and did somebody tag the goal? Hardly that. The lyric is not quite a heavenly song; the call is still out of exile to a land that is "not as others are." But in the analogy of Brown, the journey of the soul is not more often through a pathless sea than through a perpetual green pasture. Brown has said that " children are before him." If one follows his lead and learns by habit of his lore of symbol, one stands, as it were, on the edge of a shining meadow and looks ahead under the sun. There a child is planting a little flag, just a step beyond the limit of safe footing. He turns to smile with a gesture of gay bravado: " Come on! I dare you to it," he seems to say.

III

CHRISTINA ROSSETTI

I

IT was Christina Rossetti, who wrote our favourite
sonnet, though to love rather than to posterity:

> " Remember me when I am gone away,
>   Gone far away into the silent land."

We are just beginning to try, though we shall certainly not succeed. She is frankly too much for us.
She came from an unworldliness beyond our ken,
to be perceived as from another star whose light is
but coldly refracted to our own. She was, to be sure,
the natural product of those amazing Rossetti-
Polidori households, partly apprehended in the cartoon of Mr. Beerbohm, nurtured on revolutionary
ideal and hungry patriotism, on Dantesque lore
symbolic and half-occult, on religious asceticisms,
poetic fervours, self-torturing renunciations, — the
whole flavoured by the salt of the incorrigible Dante
Gabriel, alien in his temperamentalism and more
alien in his always unexpected horse-sense. She grew
up in dark houses, thirsting for light, refraining her
passionate heart and keeping it very low indeed.

Her brother's part-portrait of her as the Virgin of
the Annunciation, pure and cadaverous of design,

though not his closest likeness, restores her spirit somewhat to our imagination. We might say, however, since Christina encourages freaks of fancy, that her soul's portrait was struck out in stone some centuries ago. At least on the front of Wells Cathedral, withdrawn discreetly within her niche though exposed beyond tempering to the English winds, stands the statue of a lovely lady whom the scholars by a felicitous guess have named Saint Christina. The figure is delicate in shape, tall in emaciation, clothed in slim folds fine though severe — a cold dream of fair woman marred to sanctity. She stands sorrowful and queenly, posed lightly for all her centuries of standing, on comely and elastic foot. The head on the spare shoulders is worn by the weather, but its face is of a saint beyond a doubt, set apart from world's beauty but not forgetful of it. In her wasted hand she holds what seems to be a tablet, on which is inscribed, we may feel sure, the *De Profundis*.

Our real trouble in approaching the actual Christina of the nineteenth century is our helplessness already noted in the presence of religious poetry; for her best is most often religious. Even the love poetry, like the fine sonnet series *Donna Innominata*, is brought to the altar of religion as were her loves. And we grow increasingly squeamish over religious verse as we grow less likely to compass it for ourselves.

Our scruple is partly just. The claim to write religious poetry is always daring. English has had golden luck in the sort; but rarely have piety and poesie been found together. The mystic poet at least undertakes to say what is confessed in advance to be inexpressible. He must catch somehow a scrap of the new song reported to be sung in heaven. For religious language is seriously denatured, being commonly heard on the tongues of men and not of angels. So suspicious are we of cant in what purports to be a spiritual voice that the religious lyric must endure a more rigorous test than another. Only with reluctance will we allow it to have a genuine accent.

And Christina's non-religious verse is often tenuous enough, written in the style appropriate to a " poetess." Poesie indeed is seldom absent. Her most knowing editor has acknowledged a " film " of poetry everywhere though sometimes invisible, like the surface tension of water. These are seldom verses to be accounted negligible, worthy to be dumped into that mighty and increasing stream of verse poured out because it is easier to pour it than to write good prose. Nevertheless the mind of a " poetess " must needs go dreaming in visionary drifts of phantasy. " The Prince's Progress," " The Dead Bride," " The Lowest Room," " From House to Home " — what old-world materializations of bloodless sylph the names suggest! They swarm with prettiness and delicate vapours, " death-white " rather than " life-red " — these storied griefs and wan repinings, shaped by amorphous symbolism in a pallor of old romance. The adequate Gabriel, always his sister's best critic, wrote wisely and largely

in vain: " I wish you would try any rendering either
of narrative or of sentiment from real abundant
nature, which presents more variety even in any one
of its phases than all such " dreaming." Even " Gob-
lin Market," delightful fancy of the maiden blighted
by a feast of fairy fruit, is a symbol of its own
limitation. Fairy fruits, however luscious, have a
debilitating effect upon the human constitution, and
are in themselves not worth an honest orchard apple
or a tangible melon ripened under a cosmic sun.

The drift of reverie was all too convenient because
of Christina's facility with forms. Hers was a gift
almost unparalleled for effortless melody, for sweet-
slipping phrase and soft-falling cadence come at
simple call. We remember the family pastime of
writing sonnets in rivalry to prearranged *bouts-rimés*.
We have perhaps lingered with Christina's sonnet
of this extemporaneous birth, finished often in a few
minutes, each with its explicit sonnet form, its
natural sonnet grace, its poetic courtesy speeding
spontaneous to clarify her slightest intent. It is a
lovely ease for all its need of discipline, having no
quarrel with the trammels of the traditional meas-
ures, finding them indeed but an invitation to the
waltz. So she makes her happy or menancholy play
with the rhythms of poetry which she leads delicately forth from the long prose cadences of the
Prayer Book or the *Bible*, — the melodies as they
form the actual titles of her devotional pieces. The
good old words remain the same but set themselves
at a touch or change of syllable to liquid combina-

tions of rhythm and stanza. These have always been there, implicit, we perceive, as we watch an iambic pentameter drift lightly out of a familiar psalm-verse. A psalm, it is plain, can easily become a sonnet by a little discreet tucking and patting. Anapests can reveal themselves in the burial chant. One might suspect a sestina in the Communion, through Christina never really detached it. And ever recurring comes the chosen phrase of her soul's confession: Hope deferred maketh the heart sick.

The sorrowfulness of that refrain accounts for our reluctance to come to close quarters with this poetry. Gabriel Rossetti made his affectionate remonstrance when he wrote of help given to someone else: " I wish there were a chance of my doing the same by you, but I am afraid you find art interfere with the legitimate exercise of anguish." And to a friend: " I send you my sonnets, which are such a lively band of bogies that they may join with the skeletons of Christina's various closets." But though disease and a fantastic conscientiousness took their long turns in the miseries of Christina's days, there is no need to insist on morbidness in a life so indulgently provided with grief. Anguish for the most part was a legitimate exercise enough. We must accept it in this poetry of a solemn and ambitious maidenhood, conscious of resource, of youth forever unfulfilled, of a hard discipline calling desire back from compromise, of love which sacrificed two good lovers, one closely dear, to a fine-spun scrupulousness, of patience which watched by long death-beds

till opportunity was past, of fortitude which endured
wasting disease till beauty was consumed away, in
a life journey which wound "uphill all the way, yes,
to the very end." The verses talk of gleaming sun
and moon, but bide in a spirit-room of shadow,
watching visionary lights at distance, under a sky
which seldom transmits the comfort of a warming
day. Occasional drifts of loveliness and song pass
over,

> " As though a wind were singing,
>   High up beside the sun,"

" birds of paradise, golden, flashing," birds which
have never pecked in earthly garden, or "blessed
angels —

> Halfway between the earth and heaven
>   Joyfully borne along."

But the birds of paradise fly in a superior ether and
out of sight. The celestial singing has gone without
pause for beatitude. Back, heart, to hope deferred!
A count of the times when that theme occurs in
Christina's poetry abandons its arithmetic in the
upper decades. In brief moments the surge of desire
escapes and springs up like flame, but is sternly recalled. They have a dying fall — these cadences;
they go " plucking pale anemone," seldom " light-
ing on heartsease."

It is, however, the stark intensity of Christina's
best which is its reality. Her authentic word is no
casual utterance or " solitary recreation." It tells in

shuddering honesty of a soul's dark night sustained
through the shuttered years without persuasion of
the heavenly vision of which at least the mirage is
usually held necessary for support. It has its flashes
of assault, seeks at moments "to lay violent hands
on heaven's high treasury." But the deepest confession is of vibrant quietude, like the flaming patience of the souls in Dante's *Purgatorio* careful not
to get outside their most precious fire.

II

Christina Rossetti is the laureate of the Advent
moon. It is the moon of her birth season to which
she seems to have felt her poetry in some mystic
way committed. And the strongest reaches of her
poetic utterance, though live words, are foolishness
to readers unfamiliar with the symbolism of the
Christian year. Christina's is the season before
Christmas, when the travailing world has immemorially acknowledged the bondage of its chaos and
has waited through the ages for the coming of its
own hope deferred. Its sorrow wails in the minor
key of the old plain-song:

> "O come, O come, Emmanuel,
> And ransom captive Israel! "

It summons to ardent preparation for which the
sluggard human will must be eternally " stirred up."
" Cast away the works of darkness and put ye on
the armour of light. And having done all, stand."

So when the Advent moon first shines upon a wintry world, the " De Profundis " of her spirit begins to grope for its new music. For this solemn celebration she garnered in her symbolic treasury the figures of the watch dispersed through poetry and legend. " Behold I stand at the door and knock," saith the Lord. " I will not let thee go unless thou bless me," said Jacob having wrestled through the night with a celestial guest. Christina's central symbol is always of the midnight virgins, wise or foolish according to their wakefulness and preparation. She is never, we may be sure, in the foolish bevy with the unlit lamp, but stands steady with taper always trimmed, waiting for the bridegroom who never quite arrives in her spiritual experience though it is always " striking eleven in the courts of heaven." " Watchman, what of the night? " said the psalmist. And Christina has her answer ready, rings up on her beat, as it were, through the midnights of the years. The true watch is solitary:

" The holy cross standeth alone
  Beneath the white moon, whitest stone."

And always the music of the spheres continues the *De Profundis:* " I look for the Lord. My soul doth wait for him."

They are all in the finest Advent poem, of 1859, " The Advent moon shines cold and clear ": the nipping reality of frost, the redoubtable faith of a shivering but ready spirit, a steely quality in the verse worthy for once of the steel soul, the patience of Our

Lady of Sorrows holding spears to her breast, the deferred hope grasped for, not with the weakness of the sick-bed but with the continence which has actually preferred so to pass through things temporal as not to lose things eternal. And for once only perhaps is fellowship instead of solitude. For once above the cold of the Advent moon is a flash of authentic light from the spiritual city, though even now afar, not coming down out of heaven. Gabriel Rossetti knew what he was about when he remembered his sister in the Virgin of the Annunciation.

He should have painted her too as the Holy Child. For it is the sudden child within Christina whom we understand best, that child who consorts so oddly with the martyr of the purification and the pilgrim of the night. At Christmas, at any rate, if too rarely at other seasons, her poetry is born again to joy. Always she has kept in the palest chants of her darkest hours her swift and right naïveté of phrase, that ease of rhythm which cost her nothing, that freshness never to be captured by thought-taking, of a child's word without its fumbling or its crudity. Hence she is master-maker of Christmas carols, and is to be known at least once a year when the heart of the world remembers itself and comprehends for a fortnight the lore of innocent speech.

The child within Christina had besides her delightful secular moments. *Sing-Song Verses* are of her making, tuned and toned to a baby's ear, maybe the youngest of all child verses, dallying with the innocence of sound, playing with the single colour and the single image in a world as small as the nest. There is also the processional which enraptured Swinburne, the gentle "Pageant" of the soft-stepping months, suitable to be presented by a troupe of the holy angelicals to an audience made up entirely of Swinburnes.

Most childlike perhaps, though wise in spiritual knowledge, are the engaging volumes of devotional readings compiled from time to time and partly written by Christina, in the true tradition of the emblem. Such is the *Face of the Deep,* a devotional commentary on the Apocalypse, interpreted as an allegory in celebration of patience! — with its sweet springs of pious ejaculation, bright shoots of holy verse, with analogies of sibylline ingenuity, as pretty and decorative as the illumination in a mediaeval Book of Hours. Such is *Called to be Saints,* quaint festial of the Anglican calendar, with tasty gathering of scriptural simples, holy borrowings of sacred legend, and holy recommendations in two columns ingeniously maintained and balanced with always the right prayer for the appropriate virtue — in a simplicity rarely met since the " holy facetiousness " of the seventeenth century.

The Books of Hours, with their symmetrical flora and their innocent flexibile fauna, recall Christina's childlike friendships with all the little beasts which have meant no harm to man since a lamb " and a dove maybe," followed Eve and Adam willingly in their exile from Eden. They are an unromantic litter as they dodge in and out among the verses and the letters: the dormouse carrying his straw, the friendly lizard, the spotted toad, the attractive hedgehog, the agreeable wombat. But even the humble beasts have cognizance of the authentic saint. And we must think that the small creatures of Christina's menagerie had fellow-feeling for her, even as the seals kept still for the sermon of Columba.

Our final symbol, indeed, for the spirit of Christina before we leave her to her silent land, would best be after all a page from her *De Profundis* sweetly and joyously illuminated in shining colour and neat pattern of graceful vines and little animals after the right manner of the Book of Hours. Something as follows, let us say:

" Out of the deep have I cried unto Thee, O Lord, Lord, hear thou my voice: "

(DEVICE: a goat chasing a lamb along a ferny bed.)

" If Thou, Lord, wilt be extreme to mark what is done amiss, O Lord, who may abide it? "

(DEVICE: a squirrel cocking his tail beneath a morning-glory trellis.)

" I look for the Lord. My soul doth wait for Him."

(DEVICE: a mouse playing with a moon-beam beside a shining stone.)

" Before the morning watch, I say, before the morning watch! "

Unless we choose that the last word shall be Christina's, and a word of peace on her annual escape from Purgatory:

" O star that came out of Jacob, manifest thyself,
I entreat thee, to all the ends of the earth and
the isles of the sea. Give to each of us devotion with the shepherds and perseverance with
the magi. Add to the wisdom of the wise and
to the simplicity of the simple that single eye
that looketh unto Thee."

IV

MRS. GASKELL

I

THE fame of Mrs. Gaskell has never been be-witched to oblivion. Seldom is a writer more beloved for one book or perhaps for two. But if we will trouble ourselves to rummage among her plentiful writings, we come with odd regret, as at a pleasure almost missed, upon a multitude of stories dear to her contemporaries, known to us only in name or perhaps not at all. We find them pale from long sojourn in the dark places of neglect — but still alive with a curious modernity of power set in a quaintness of style and taste. Here is a world unquestionably of the past, more evasive than the strong, hurtling clamour of Scott, the full-peopled bustle of Dickens, the prim outrageousness of the Brontës, or the bright, sane days behind Jane Austen's window. But it is a world in itself which seems to touch, by a strange contradiction, the borders of the eighteenth and the twentieth centuries.

At our first stroll beyond the close-hedged paths of Cranford, the voices of the past sound far clearer than the complex medley of to-day. We are in an authentic world of human folk but not a part of it, present at actual doings and yet invisible, as some of

us feel with our glasses on. But we need the glasses;
it is hard even then to realize that Mrs. Gaskell be-
longs to the heyday of the modern novel. And our
sense of anachronism comes naturally from her limitation. Her great contemporaries kept for the most
part somewhat in advance of their age, since the
native way of genius is to pioneer, to push ahead
of public demand. How else would come the necessary friction to light its path? But Mrs. Gaskell is apt
to show a singular pliancy, bending with intuitive
suavity to the predilections of her readers, to those
secret indulgences of which they are perhaps unconscious, modestly regardless, at least in early years,
that her own instinct would be a better guide. Dickens might carry the public by storm, Thackeray
sting it to a healthy resentment; but in so far as it
was well-disposed, Mrs. Gaskell, delicately sensitive
to circumstance and environing influence, would con-
form to it with a gracious and yielding complaisance.
Hence appears in her work that contradiction of
retrocession and progress, of vagueness and distinction of aim, which baffles an attempt at strict
analysis, except in so far as it is found always feminine, refined by a high-bred and effective womanhood.

The quaintness is only superficially a matter of
style, though the mild euphemisms of our grand-
mothers mix easily with the flow of her strong facility.
The sun still " drives his chariot up into the azure
heavens," and " his fiery-footed steeds gallop apace

toward the close of a happy day." The trees " don " their leaves as if for the first time, and " a perfect bridal of the earth and sky " is a frequent occurrence. Death is a " sure balm," or again a " beautiful messenger to bring the weary home." But all this is merely Mrs. Gaskell's pretty deference to the phraseology of her elderly readers.

We may understand her better after one quiet morning with the crumbling old reviews, which, more exactly than novels, reveal the changing mode of literary opinion. Perhaps we smile a little at the comments upon *Ruth* and *Mary Barton,* the only novels of our author which seem to have made a " stir " among the magazines, but the smile is not in scorn but in refreshment.

They wrote good articles in the old fifties — that was a matter of common acceptance. Sir Oracle was still undisturbed in his high calling; he took himself quite seriously; he did not for a moment doubt that he would be believed. He was withal full master of his language. Yet his authoritative assertions startle our present habits of thought like the slight thrill of a dim returning memory, so youthful sounds this unabashed self-confidence of eighty years ago. There breathes in the faded pages a responsive energy of expression, an abounding ardour of missionary utterance which seems juvenile to our more wary modernism. Airily, or with portentous state, justice is meted, but it is an artless justice, delighting in the command of critical prattle but for all its bravery of carriage sometimes disregardful for the sanctities of form, the essence of which current criticism supposes itself to be brewed.

They took the story as a personal matter — hence our immediate sense of the naïve. For we used to think a little after that fashion ourselves in vivid childhood days. Did we like a book? That was the question. Did the characters suit our fancy? Was the hero supremely generous and martyr-like? Was the heroine most divinely fair? Should we prefer to be married to Sir Kenneth of Scotland or to Mr. Darcy of Pemberley? The stories were our stories by a quick adoption, their people our most familiar friends. Shame befall the author who should disappoint our zeal for first-class humanity! All very foolish, no doubt. The comparison would grossly insult Mrs. Gaskell's sprightly critics, for though their point of view may be often puerile, their comprehension is uniformly mature. But their fiction world too was delightfully real, and they too preferred it as far as possible unblemished.

In the creation of women, at least, they found Mrs. Gaskell perhaps over ready to oblige them. Her maidens move in a surpassing loveliness, till one admirer owns that praise may have a limit. We are more awake to the flaw to-day, now that it has grown unseemly for a novelist to laud his own creations, just as it is no longer mannerly to boast of one's own children. It is permissible to dress them well, to invite company to see them, to let them talk as much as they please — but praise must work by suggestion;

never must it be boldly said that they surpass in attractions and accomplishments all other young ladies in town. Not so with Mrs. Gaskell. If her literary daughters have faults of form, those faults will ne'er be known. There is the fallen Ruth, type of almost uncanny refinement; her face "positively Greek," with "proud and superb turn of head, a spiritual look in her eyes that made you wonder at their depths — a clear ivory skin as smooth as satin, her hair grown darker and deeper in the shadow that lingered in its masses." There is the statuesque Margaret Hale of *North and South,* accustomed to stand in the presence of her manly lover, "her throat curved outwardly like a swan's, her eyelids drooped half over her eyes, her teeth shut, not compressed, her lips just parted over them, allowing the white lines to be seen between their curves, her slow, deep breathing dilating her beautiful nostrils, her head thrown backward in the old proud attitude, her hair jet black, her clear, smooth skin" — and if there be any other good features, she has them. We are almost repelled at such amateur union of the mawkish and the sensuous, but a better mind returns with the memory of wayward Sylvia, nice Molly Gibson, and the field freshness of the country Phillis, wholesome as a misty apple. And, remembering them, we will forgive the others the excellence of their beauty. At any rate we will not wish ourselves quite back in to-day, when heroines are so likely to come over thirty, and be fat or wrinkled or married.

In 1853 the public was still content with charming

girls, content with whatever Mrs. Gaskell gave them, if indeed the reviewers set the standard as absolutely as they judged. Perhaps it was lucky for her that she lived, even though hampered by old models, in an age of artistic discovery. A writer is surer of considerate welcome when great things are found a matter of course and a full-fledged genius is expected any day. The excitement was still keen at new anomalies, *Vanity Fair* without a hero, *Jane Eyre* with uncomely heroine, at the " humane and prodigious triumph in the actuality of modern fiction," " its emancipation from the stage setting of novels." The critic could afford to be complacent, to run a riot of wantonly rejoicing similes in the abundance of such superior pickings. In April, 1853, George Henry Lewes begins as follows: " The whole force of English romance writing has been deployed during the last six months. Dickens, Thackeray, Bulwer, the chiefs of that department of literature, have been in full play; and Miss Brontë, Mrs. Gaskell, Mrs. Marsh, Mrs. Gore, Miss Julia Kavanagh, and lesser ladies, have advanced platoon-wise and almost simultaneously discharged each a new volume." Such promiscuous classification seems well devised to punish the vanity of the exclusive, but to others it offered safety. In such high company Mrs. Gaskell was assured of respect with so many " lesser ladies " in contrast.

The praise of her, all pitched to that comfortable degree, the superlative, has the deference of an old-fashioned courtliness, quite innocent of desire to put the " lady novelist " in her place. Shakespeare himself, it seems agreed, was " not more dramatically inspired in the presentation of character." Her people are " difficult to portray as ever novelist attempted," " her success great as ever novelist achieved." Around the death-bed of Ruth " flits the shadow of Ophelia." " Consummate " and " exquisite " perfection is easily accorded to Ruth's creator.

II

Her purity of moral appeal her admirers valued most dearly. For though the purpose novel was already a storm centre, fiction for the common need must be by common consent a resource " for doing God's work on earth." When Mrs. Gaskell trenched on social grounds and tried with feminine tact to cut the barrier between capital and labour, there was a twitter of alarm. What if she should spread too far afield the conviction that the labourer worthy of his hire is not always plump and contented? But with morality and holiness she is allowed to be wholly within her sphere. The garment of righteousness is always becoming. The lady novelist must " write in the fear of God," must " take her calling as an author in Christian earnest," that she may be " a rock " to wayfarers " wearied with the greatness of their way." Old-fashioned criticism, indeed!

Canonical or not, such appreciation was unlikely to improve the work of Mrs. Gaskell, already exemplary enough. It was only too easy for her to continue the Edgeworth tradition of the "moral tale" since her nimble dexterity, a thrifty virtue which may lean toward failing's side, achieved with slight effort a deft distinctness of finish, and developed perhaps too far a preference for the unmistakable in characterization. Such a style is dangerously apt for reformatory purposes. Virtuous intent could perhaps be allowed. There are some of us even now who can win through, unspotted, to the end of a moral tale. The real complaint is not that the tale is moral, but that it is too obvious, that it sets gratuitously forth the essential secrets of fiction. Who cares for a puzzle all worked out, or a riddle tagged with its answer? This neglect of the shadow and insistence on the high light mars some valuable work of Mrs. Gaskell long after she has learned to wear her Christian calling less anxiously.

She does dearly love to reclaim the erring. Who could delay to repent and sign the pledge after reading the story of pious little Tom Fletcher, who converted and transformed an entire demoralized family by the persuasion of infant rectitude? And there is staunch little Maggie of *The Moorland Cottage*, good among a hundred torments, slighted by a partial mother, hectored by a horrid brother, who jumps out of the swing and hits his sister and doesn't mind. No wonder that, growing hardened in sin, he almost wrecks poor Maggie's life. He drowns, observe, at the crucial moment. These are telling warnings. We must hasten to "go after the good and leave the evil." But let us submit ourselves and mend our ways if we are beginning to laugh. Mrs. Gaskell has often the charm of a child-like guilelessness, but more seldom than most people is she absurd. And there is still something to be said for fiction which strives consciously " to do God's work on earth," though not just what was said by Mrs. Gaskell's godly critics.

Unlike us, however, they are sure to find the saving grace most free in passages of fulsome pathos, to return a spontaneous commendation for stories " tearfully interesting," whose pity " searches out the tears that hide away from men's eyes in their hearts and moistens the sympathy that generally dries up in the whirl of events, and, pulverized in the dust of sentimentality, blows blindingly away." The metaphor is intricate; the writer must be much moved. The editorial eye, one would guess, could in those days always be blinded by a tear.

Along just this track we seem to have travelled farthest since early Victorian days. We have grown excessively shy of open sentiment. English literature used of old to glory in its sensibility since first Griselda was brought from Italy to be cried over. But now we no longer like to cry in company. If a piteous tale is really too much for us, we must pretend that something ails our eyes. We have come a long way since the flower of English society rejoiced to lift up its voice in concert at the unspeakable misfortunes of Clarissas and Angelinas, long even since it felt the better for a quiet weep at the homelier troubles of Mrs. Gaskell's Ruths and Sylvias, Maggies and Jemimas.

Here, with her earnestness for "the human with its droppings of warm tears," Mrs. Gaskell is the truest daughter of her time. If we have tears, we must look to our eyes, for lamentable things are to be witnessed. We watch helplessly at the deaths of happy children, noisy an hour ago; at the despair of the fierce grown tame by suffering; at poverty glooming in silent rage by the slow starvation of its dear ones; at innocence betrayed to a terrible patience of unremitting punishment; at blighted youth waiting cheerfully the approach of blindness, solitude, infirmity, disgrace; at the inarticulate broodings of bewildered age; at whatever sorrow is most unbearable to see because meekly borne by the sufferer. Nor can we take our usual comfort when we wake from the dream, that it never happened. It happened; for Mrs. Gaskell, even in her most dolorous vein, is a maker of real people, a considerable genius in the age which triumphed in "the actuality of modern fiction."

Her unsparing tenderness, always poignant and appealing, never contemptible, does sometimes exceed the modesty of nature. It may be that the world has not grown hard-hearted — has learned only a reticence necessary to art. The fervent spinning of a long agony intrudes on the privacy of pain. We seem like spectators pausing from curiosity at an accident. We feel a little vulgar; if we can do nothing about it, we ought to pass on. Certainly Mrs. Gaskell is not here at her best. She knew well how to develop the logic of experience, to make a moral result sufficient punishment for a cause of weakness; yet was too often willing to drag a chain of fortuitious calamity, "plague, pestilence, and famine, battle, murder, and sudden death." Thick crowding griefs, we must admit besides, either precipitate a not too healthy excitement, or else lose their significance. Outraged feeling must rebel and slacken under a strain too tense. Such a reaction cools our sympathy before the final fever which rounds the tale of Ruth's martyrdom; at the death-bed of John Barton, where murderer and avenger unite in a rapture of self-abnegation; even for Sylvia's husband, who returns, defaced, reviled, stripped of all but heart-hunger, to lurk unseen about the cheer of his forbidden home. Pity strides the air too rampantly.

But Mrs. Gaskell doubtless knew what she was about, believing rightly that only by development of her understood powers could she wake into use the dormant qualities of her genius. Pathos is the low-built foundation of her art; without it the world would never have come to love her for a gentle lady with a merry heart. Seeking acquaintance with diversity of grief, but listening and alert for better news of herself, she followed with energy a lively series of experiments, sometimes failing, sometimes succeeding, but working, although by no means steadily, towards a more complete freedom of faculty. An unusual amplitude of scope is evident from the first. In her early popular novels, *Mary Barton* and *North and South*, she can claim a sympathetic and unprejudiced intelligence for the struggles between the

labourer and the employer. Sometimes she skirts the
edge of a darker field, though lacking as a rule command of the stern silences. So in *A Dark Night's
Work* the secret of hidden crime waits its revelation
with punishment terribly out of proportion to the
original guilt. In *The Doom of the Griffiths* there
passes through the gloomy quarrel of father and son
a faint foreshadow of Stevenson. And at least in
Sylvia's father, Daniel Robson, surly, dogged York-
shireman, rude creature of his bleak home, stubborn
unto death, she reaches near the inner circle of that
miserable tragedy of stupidity, more strongly treated
by the greater George Eliot.

Once by an amusing accident, in *The Grey
Woman,* she produces a tale not of pity but of terror,
well worth reading as a contribution to the list of
tremors which English fiction has offered for cure
of the man who knew not how to shiver. If that
dullard remained impassive before *The Castle of
Otranto* and the *Romance of the Forest,* let him try
this. He will feel a sensation, I promise him, though
he have blindly refused to shudder at giant helmets
fallen from heaven, at Titan limbs protruding from
unused halls, at fate hid in auger-holes, or groans
behind thick masonry. For here is a pale and terrible
husband who out-Bluebeards Bluebeard, a grim land
of castle and mill, where hunted ladies, crawling
under tables, hit against corpses which should not be
there, or gaze from lofts upon pursuers ramping below. And the scroll: "*Ainsi les chasseurs se ven-
gent!*" How is that? Let the purveyors of horror

look to their fame! And Mrs. Gaskell has known
better than most how to base her wildness on the
commonplace, for she starts on her witch flight
through haunted air from a real inn kitchen, oppressively bright and hot, and crowded with folks hurrying in from the rain.

But a blood-boltered narrative at best could be for
Mrs. Gaskell only an adventure. She was prompt to
learn that her feet were straying if they passed along
ungentle ways. And so, in quest of her peculiar need,
she half divined from the first art's ancient platitude,
soon quickened by experience, that tears, pure and
clean, dry best in laughter's light. Accepting her
mission to be the voice of pity's entreaty, she found
pity's answer in the reaction of loving mirth, which
is pity's release and escape. For clean laughter has
held the comfort to sanctify sorrow since first
Demeter laughed in the pain of bereft motherhood at
the simplicity of a familiar thing. In her best hours,
therefore, Mrs. Gaskell read clearly the crystal of
her genius, knew that she was born under the dancing
star, able to heal pain's bitterness by her dainty
cheer of heartsease. She had come to her individual
world where " even the wise " do well to be merry of
heart.

III

The grace to detect the little springs of laughter's
source was the sure result of her fundamental excellence, through which she is, in a measure, always
great and always modern, — her instinct for the

significant detail. Even in the most searching of her
pathetic appeals the sincerest " tears of things " are
tears of the little things. Not at her scenes of excessive pain do we shrink, which, ruthless in their extremity of grief, yet fail of tragedy's reserve. It is
harder to notice Jem's pockets, bulging with oranges
for the stricken children, or Alice Wilson's loving
fingers as she handles the box packed for her by her
mother so many years ago. Under a reverent tenderness the least of small trifles takes a clinging value,
like a broken relic used long ago by hands now quiet.
It touches the heart like a tale of past youth told by
firelight in the gloaming. But the touch is kindliest
when the tale is of Mrs. Gaskell's best, a merry one
for all its memories, sweet and wise in the lore of
love.

Her cheer is but the eternal relish for the discovery
of common traits of nature drawn again with the fine
clearness of porcelain. A life may be infinitely pitiful
and infinitely absurd, so fragile, so unreasonable, so
genuine. To recognize the human truth of an oddity
in character or situation is to have a good jest for
ever. Hence the wholly winsome laughter which
saves and corrects the sentimentality of the early
Cranford — at a familiar foible, a meek stubborn-
ness, a serene prejudice, a shrinking delicacy, faint as
an aged scent. So in exceeding feebleness of yearning
grief dear Miss Mattie burns her treasure of old
letters but saves candles the while with exemplary
economy. So, rebellious to the order of immediate
frugality, proud Martha marches into the dining-

room, triumphant with her lion pudding. So, when the poor ladies resolve on the hard sacrifice of money for Miss Martha's support, Miss Pole spares our quivers by the admirable formality of her set speech. From school-days we have been brought up on *Cranford*, thin bread and butter, brooches, and all. We have loved each simple faith and fancy unbreakable but fine with the daintiness of gossamer, its subtleties of undoubted etiquette, the quaint guises of its ignorance, its meagre comforts, its shy secrets over recipes or long-withered loves, its placid blindness to poverty's makeshifts, its kindness. But how should we love *Cranford* if we did not smile? And again, in that more farcical Cranford, the Duncombe of *Dr. Harrison's Confessions*, the laugh rings clear, like a sweet field wind. But it rings always low with the self-effacement of high breeding, for Mrs. Gaskell never shows more mirth than she is mistress of. Only she is learning the mellow wisdom of England's first lover of pathos, that " litel hevinesse " is quite enough for most folks.

Instinct, again, rather than deliberate effort, guided Mrs. Gaskell's fine choice of pictorial setting. Tireless ever in her zest for detail, exquisitely responsive to sense impression, she could create a convincing rightness of surrounding, imagined with the force of a lesser Hardy. Her creatures, too, move close to the ground in a wholesome kinship with the powers of the air and the beasts of the field. But her earth, though checkered by bleak moors and gale-swept solitudes, is not the mother of human sorrow, waiting to call back to obscure burial the little lives she has put forth. It is an earth of perpetually-moving light, of shade in the flight of sunshine, of scudding gust and changing gleam, of cloud-shadows creeping sideways on a warm hill, of purple darkness chased by amber glow. Hers, too, is the strong pulse of physical perception, an alertness to sight and sound, and especially to touch, as if each sense were for the moment alone, dependent on itself. There is the feel of the wind on the face, gentle with rain or brisk with sea challenge, a strong pull of rope on the arm, the prickle of gorse on the ankle. Herein lies her escape from triviality in the rare firmness of her pastoral, the almost elemental simplicity of her country scenes, like the favourite *Cousin Phillis,* where love and prayer, apple-gathering and harvesting, go on against the grey of the beeches and the blue of the sky. With all her inclination for the elegant refinements she has usually the wit to prefer the homely, to bid us notice the green track left by the cat in the grey of the dewy grass, " the small, bright insects which run hither and thither on the elastic flower-stems," the milkpans sweetening in the sun, the pad of the crisp young peas as they fall, the radiation of warmth to meet an indoor chill.

Peculiarly precious to Mrs. Gaskell seems the suggestion of an interior. At times she shows an almost Dutch appreciation for the effect of light and colour beyond a foreground of shade, a vista through cool rooms and opening casements of a bright old-fashioned garden, of sunshine on the slope of an orchard wall, overhung by awkward limbs of jargonelle pear, with a lithe Sophie below tilting for the fruit. All the better does she love to linger within, if the room be worn and set in permanent character by generations of use, quiet with the stillness of aged houses — has perhaps a stretch of flag-stone floor, broad window seats, and diamond panes, and low-roofed passages at irregular levels. But such age is never defaced with ruin; rather is it alive with hope, searched through by the thrill of children's voices, trodden by small feet which step lightly upon memory's trace.

For the human detail, the separate flavour and importance of each private experience, became with Mrs. Gaskell's growth of supreme importance to her. She would be hurt to know herself classed to-day somewhat as an antiquarian novelist, a lover of the old and the odd for the sake of age and oddity. Age was venerable to a mind like hers, if only as a shade of past life, sanctified by a gathering cluster of intimate associations; but age was readily absorbing to her artist self just because the habit of time sharpens and simplifies a personality to a clarity of distinctness. For the same cause she delighted in an eccentricity, not as an accident but as an accentuation of humanity. We have noticed already her precision of character delineation, exaggerated sometimes to a fault. But we should sorely miss the lively company of souls dear and queer who bustle cheerfully about their business in her brisk little world. By no means all live in Cranford. There are the peering Miss

Brownings of Hollingford, the whimsically benign
Lady Ludlow, the Sidebothams, blindly devoted to
their one devotion, the unalterable Morton sisters,
Miss Annabella, Miss Sophronia, Miss Cordelia —
excuse me, I should have mentioned Miss Sophronia
first. Better are the highly-marriageable ladies of
Duncombe, Mrs. Rose, the Bullocks, the Thomkin-
sons. And there is no trace at all of the fantastic in
the lusty flock of minor characters who form a teeming background to the woes of our unfortunate heroines; the dogged servants, Martha, Sally, old Kester,
the sallow shop-tenders, the simple country folk so
diverse and so real. Full-blooded are they all; not
even one to be mistaken for a property figure.

So to Mrs. Gaskell there was opening a broader,
firmer art, where " warm tears " should at last have
no occasion to drop, an art comfortable, leisurely,
sane with a genial and cleanly tolerance. Such is the
fuller humanity of the unfinished *Wives and Daughters,* well stocked with a normal and pleasant society
of worthy folks, not too clearly marshalled after
their kind but uncommonly interesting to know.
They seldom expose themselves to our pity or
laughter, for they have learned to put a good face
forward, and usually to smile at their own folly. If
any turn out to be old friends met before in Mrs.
Gaskell's society, we are all the better pleased, more
especially as they are plainly improved by the experience. There is the refined and ailing lady, frequently married by Mrs. Gaskell to a stolid yeoman,
strong, loving, stubborn. The ubiquitous gossips are

probably incapable of change. But at last appears an excellent country doctor, witty, self-respecting, sensible gentleman, and some very likable young men who have outgrown the school-girl glibness of Mrs. Gaskell's early volubility. And the amiable county family is quite new, new too, bright, volatile Cynthia, admirable foil for our steady Molly, new and all but perfect the specious refinements of the sentimental step-mother. The portraiture of experience is unfailingly sympathetic. We all remember an agony of childish self-consciousness like Molly's first visit to the Hall: " She had to sit very forward to avoid crushing the Miss Brownings' new dresses, and yet not too forward for fear of incommoding fat Mrs. Goodenough and her niece; and, to add to her discomfort, Molly felt herself very conspicuously placed in the middle of the carriage." More than once, too, have we seen just the offended dignity of poor Mr. Cox's calf-love:

MR. GIBSON: " To convey a letter clandestinely to my daughter, a mere child! "

MR. COX: " Miss Gibson, sir, is nearly seventeen. I heard you say so yourself only the other day! "

We know how they feel, dear human friends, through all the seven ages. And we have to leave them not quite settled; there is a real sore, for we " like them " very much. " Such a disappointment," said a loving essay published at Mrs. Gaskell's death, " is one of the highest testimonies to a writer's genius."

We shall not find anything more simple or more true to say. If we would know the inwardness of Mrs. Gaskell's charm, we must go back to the critical naïveté of her time, for more kingdoms than the kingdom of Heaven are open only to hearts of children. Nor is it hard for us to feel the necessary guilelessness, for our curiosity is altogether unaffected. I should like to hear quite told the story of Cambuscan and know for certain who had Canace to wife. There are other secrets which shall ever lie hidden — what dread discovery awaited Edwin Drood above the winding stair, by what stoutness of heart Denis Duval achieved the winning of his Agnes, with what wildness of human despair Weir of Hermiston fulfilled his doom by the Weaver's Stone. But if I could choose my story, I would rather be present some sunny morning at the wedding of Roger and Molly. I would stay to the breakfast — to marvel at mamma's roseate blandishments, to hear Lord Cumnor ask questions, and learn by what sage effort of humorous common sense the doctor resigned himself to the loss of his Molly. We can foresee their future as clearly as we used to know for the hundredth time the coming fate of Little Red Riding-hood. But just the same, " please tell us how it ended."

V

THE PROSE OF MR. BEERBOHM

I

TO look back over Mr. Beerbohm's prose is not to renounce our hopes for its future. Mr. Beerbohm represents no longer, to be sure, " the younger generation knocking at the door." But he has by no means shut the door behind him. Precedence in the door-way will probably be long accorded to him by successive crops of " *les jeunes* " growing up around. We may count on a volume of personal essays to be called perhaps *After All,* to succeed the *Works, More, Yet Again, And Even Now,* and *A Variety of Things,* unless *Around Theatres* be that volume under another name. But Mr. Beerbohm's work of late years has been so much more representative as cartoonist than as essayist, except in the salvaging of older material, that we are justified in regarding the past garnerings of prose as something special and nearly complete in themselves. Criticism can now find the genial excuse of amusement recollected in tranquillity. And it is getting to feel a little easier therefore.

For there has always been something a bit wary about the printed word on Mr. Beerbohm's prose. Few, one surmises, have felt perfectly comfortable in the analysis of this tenuous thing with its engaging air of harmlessness. Mr. Beerbohm, therefore, except when he has ventured to sharpen unhallowed pencil at Labour or at the Lord's Anointed, has perhaps endured too little " the unexempt condition " healthy for writers. At simplest there has always been the risk of taking raillery for earnest. We Philistines like our distinctions clear cut; we like things good or bad, healthy or poisonous, beautiful or ugly, serious or funny. Mr. Beerbohm, however, has seldom obliged us by initial clue; and hence the alarm before the spot-light, his chosen emblem, which shoots so clear a shaft. The critic suffers a sort of psychic uneasiness, with fellow-feeling for the criminal of the detective story whose picture is taken from behind by some invisible exposure.

The critic cannot play his first trick. He cannot in the handy old way relate this prose to something else. It has its sure limitations of style and sympathy, but it carries some private insurance against analogical impertinence. The pleasant autobiographical phantasy, " Diminuendo," probably truer than it pretends to be, remembers the boy's reverence for the Pater cult, but makes a brilliant bolt from any Pater discipleship. The early choice of all artifice to be Mr. Beerbohm's province suggests the Wilde formula, but his preciosities have always been made of sterner stuff than were Wilde's. He has praised the excellent prose of Whistler, and certain passages of his essay on Whistler might be taken to define a capacity of his own, but how different his other capacities! Frequently a seemingly irrelevant memory of Sterne drifts through the mind as one follows the Beerbohm pages — of that other "pose-fancier" of long ago, dedicated to the technique of the trifle, to the exploitation of a pleasant ego, to what Mr. Beerbohm has called an "elastic subtlety of phrase." But Sterne had no elastic subtlety of thought to bequeath to his heirs. Recurrently too we remember Thackeray, Thackeray the Roundabout, — his lucky style which Mr. Beerbohm has well honoured, his phrase *juste* although garrulous, the knack at turning to use a swarm of autobiographical amenities. But Mr. Beerbohm's memories by no means swarm and his word comes by no means of itself, as he has complained to his readers more than once. We recall last Mr. Beerbohm's witty remembrance of a Maupassant discipleship, his youthful ardour for wrought simplicity. But his most natural praises have been for a George Meredith or a Henry James.

With his sheer nonsense, in which of course he is extremely neat, we know where we are. But that inverted sort of thing was more entertaining to the "child author" of the nineties who would construct with clever pains a formal essay on the technique of complete dandyism or the aesthetic of incendiary fires. The form of topsy-turvy, the elevation of a minor mood to the place of common sense, is an art indeed, perhaps with Mr. Beerbohm a fine art. But its best creator in literary form is the spirit which is in some sense an "innocent." And Mr. Beerbohm, even as the child author, was always astute as the most elderly changeling.

We know where we are too with the confessed parodies. The form was apt for Mr. Beerbohm, since it is at once subtle and simple — infinitely capable of distinct perfection but not explaining itself, a delight to whoso can take it, a blank for whoso must leave it. Caricature, as Mr. Beerbohm writes it, accords with his theory for caricature as he draws it — being "on a fine scale, an exaggeration of the whole creature from top to toe, without intentional altering of the proportions," preserving as it can the values of the thing upon which it fastens.

Old magazine files still hold the spark of many lost bits of parody which Mr. Beerbohm otherwise thrifty in literary salvage has chosen to let go, such as his first dramatic criticism for the *Saturday Review,* in which Pinero and Mr. Comyns-Carr agree upon collaboration in a delightful frisk of Jacobean dialogue. In the amusing "Savonarola" an "Elizabethan play," most Italians known to fame from the thirteenth to the sixteenth centuries circulate in a pleasant jumble of murder, tag-quotation, and anachronism. In the *Christmas Garland,* we agree, are met in singular naturalness all the Parnassian company of our modern prose writers, each delightfully "bedevilled," each delightfully possessed of his faculties and his authentic voice. *Zuleika Dobson,* that bright though protracted Iliad of youth and love and Oxford town, takes the risk of every extended

tour de force: " Excep' when awful long I've found
it good." But here is the variety which goes with good
caricature. We follow the extravaganza of love always seeking repulse; we adore the face of Zuleika,
that modern Helen, the face that launched a thousand
youths to drown for her in the Isis, and draped with
black the memorable towers of Oxford. But there
is a network of other trivialities at Oxford, noted and
exaggerated with the perspicacity of common-sense.
Everywhere protrudes the base of the silly, the
simple, the mawkish, the sordid, the matter-of-fact,
— the natural milieu of frenzy and sentiment. Here
is good parody. But there is better floating vaporous
among the informalities of Mr. Beerbohm's more
serious work, the personal essay.

II

Here at home on its own preserve the wit evades
by its simplicity. Where to take hold? It is not easy
to salt the tail of this bird, ever slipping on to the
next twig, commonly chirping only once in a spot,
leaving the pursuer in an awkward pose. Its suavity
beguiles. Pure and innocent, it pursues its confession,
though that confession may be specious. It steps
lightly on its little journeys, starting little trails of
irrelevance and inadvertency. A whiff of parody stirs
about a little while and then drifts away. There shines
a sparkle at the sudden meeting of sense and absurdity. A paradox, carefully unprepared for, flashes and
is gone. We enter, unsuspecting, the ambush of an

apparently ingenuous confidence, but a haunting cadence wakes for a second the suspicion of raillery
and leaves us uncertain. It is irreproachable in tone
but has the mocking correctness of the echo.

Mr. Beerbohm's best irony is, of course, trim and
trained, a nicety of casualness. It beguiles by a consistency of undertoning. Not that it is always at its
best. The youthful dramatic critic fulfilling his Saturday Reviewish stint of impudence, could seem subtle
only after the tonic outrageosities of G. B. S. And
the assured author of today who jeers at his readers
in prefaces or at Americans in tangents, though welcome to any personal liberty that he may be taking, is
less welcome to the obviousness of the way. But complaint is churlish, so much more frequent is our delight in the polished economy of stroke. Such irony
is, as its maker would have it, "little sister of restraint," agreeably seen as a little sister should be,
but never clamorously heard.

In his best essay manner, for instance, is the little
masterpiece, "Quia Imperfectum," an apparently
reverent meditation upon a detail of Goethe's biography, in fact ingenious satire upon the Goethe egotism, bland and leisurely in play about the unruffled
surface of the great Olympian. Here and there in the
Goethe letters is reference to a certain Tischbein who
once began to paint a portrait of Goethe in the romantic manner and for some reason left the work
unfinished — that is all. And upon this base Mr.
Beerbohm's fancy gravely circles in deferential and
tireless speculation, reading between the lines, as it

were. No fault is hinted, no dislike so much as hesi-
tated. The essay supposes, expounds, relates, inter-
prets, regrets. The foolish face of praise does not
even once peep baldly through the irony.

Parable is an equally happy shape, and equally
elusive. For good parable may be a miracle of harmlessness, where the artist, if he be artist enough,
joins the touch of a child and of the serpent. Most
perfect, most painful, for instance, is the sorrowful
" Something Defeasible," in which without too obvious symbolism the baffled conservative wonders at
the popular willingness to scrap the structures which
the centuries have been a-building. We stand in the
story among children playing by the sea, and frater-
nize with an attractive boy, wise, discreet, silent,
who builds his sand castle like an artist and a friend
of man, but when the waves come, delights with a
sheer relish for catastrophe which is special to our
age or maybe common to eternal man. Less good,
though not less entertaining, is the " Dreadful
Dragon " of *A Variety of Things*, satire on the Brit-
ish character in its wartime psychology, seen in abo-
riginal simplicity centuries before London was, hear-
ing of foreign dragons as legendary things without
fear lest they invade the immune islet, betrayed to
panic and then rallying to good behaviour at smoke
from a real dragon, relaxed at the dragon's death to
decadent laxity and solemn iconoclasm, restored to
form by the hoax of a sham dragon efficacious as
was the real upon the public spirit.

The sham dragon recalls Mr. Beerbohm's lifelong

preoccupation with shams and surfaces, his amusement over form without content, over the image without life. Here are faces which are masks and masks which are faces. He is curious and ever entertained about wax-work shows, the doings of unsubstantial royalty, the wiggery of the law-courts, the perfection of the dandy's outside, the recurrent rocking-horse on which, spite of his sophistication, Mr. Beerbohm has evidently had in his time many a glorious ride. We descend to subterranean crypts to ponder before the effigies of defunct magnificoes, which are crumbling obscurely to an imitation dust. Mr. Beerbohm, whether or not we suspect him of derision, likes a good surface for its own sake and never denies that the very mask attracts him. Here is no Carlylese impatience with flummeries and forms. The modern Sartor Resartus is a Tailor Retailored with elegance and satisfaction. Still one wonders.

Most characteristic is the merry parable of the *Happy Hypocrite,* the love-tale of an old roué who to wed his purest Jenny, actress undefiled, has bought and worn the face of a saint, — has worn it securely till the devil one day, bent on exposure, rips the mask from its place, and — lo — beneath, the face of a saint indeed. Here is, belike, in the irony, the shadow of our human masquerade, our filagree aims, our filagree ends. Here is, just as likely, the hope of our dreams; for if saints there be, and perhaps there be, they are made only in this way. Imp or moralist the author must be, we say, and perhaps most nearly one when he pretends the other. But there is something restful in this appealing sprite, unknown to the devil and his enemy.

III

The personality, fictitious or not, which the essays present, is carefully toned down to a finesse of moderation. It was unnecessary to announce that it would not be of the "plungingly intimate kind." Though it insists upon a disarming vanity, it is for the most part unofficious, with one positive assertion — a distaste for "vibrancy" in any form, whether in martyr or hygiene enthusiast. The satire on Pater makes humorous renouncement of "sensations," "pulsations," and "exquisite moments." It fully intends *not* to be "present at the focus where the greatest number of forces unite in their purest energy." The same tone appears in the capital little essay, "The Crime," wherein the author, spending the evening alone in a borrowed room, tries vainly in a spurt of daring to burn a volume by a lady novelist solemn in her intellects and strong with that serious vitality which makes cowards of all the rest of us.

Certainly the ego of the essays is conservative. It would hardly possess its peculiar gifts did it not belong to the Intelligentsia mentioned by Plato, who stand aside from the press and keep themselves neat and clean. "On the banner that I wave is embroidered a device of prunes and prisms," wrote the "child author" when he was still official spokes-

man for the younger generation. And the cartoonist
of recent years has had sad and sometimes unwelcome wisdom, unsweetened by any special hope to
set the crooked straight. And despite the sorrowful
keenness of recent cartoons, victims who have complained of cruelty have had sometimes a passable
case, since their bedevilment has lacked now and
then the zest and irresponsibility which Mr. Beerbohm has required of good caricature. The Beerbohm
essay, too, despising heroics in a world gone mad or
vulgar, has approached the depths with some resentment, leaving us undecided as to what depths there
are. But strictures here would be specially unimagi-
native, since we know that Mr. Beerbohm dislikes
the friendly shoulder-patting of the English personal
essay: "How detestable the writer who obviously
touts for our affection, arranging himself for us in a
mellow light." No, the Beerbohm essay never makes
" a blatant bid for love."

Friendly and knowing it is, none the less, especially in the middle volumes. There is a nice little
glow within the sparkle. There is sociability as well
as warning in the urbane platitude, " Every human
being repays attention." And in the genial confes-
sional appear those touches of nonsense in human psychology which makes the whole world kin. They peer
at us under the excellent manipulation: the child-
games we play in our elderly heads, our likings for
our little comforts, " our innate passion for breaking records," our cobweb frauds, our comic lassi-
tudes, our gushes of untimely intimacy, our stiffen-

ings of untimely reticence, our infections of oratory,
our irrational timidities, our irrational distastes, our
furtive and elaborate vanities, our drifts of sentiment, our ready sympathies when there is no occasion for them.

Upon these sympathies, nevertheless, Mr. Beerbohm very cleverly plays. He has sustained a lifelong jibe at Victorian sentimentalism, but it would
be possible for a sufficiently bold blade to write an
essay on Max Beerbohm the Sentimentalist. Material
would lie at hand in the unusual sketch, "William
and Mary," idyl of one year's love and sweet marriage in a Joyous Garde of a cottage — gone save for
the ringing of a bell in an empty hall, like the ghost
of a remembered laugh. For once we prepare to shed
the licensed tear. But on second thought we suspend
it, guessing that we and the tale are undergoing a
psychological test to determine how much we will
stand. Our gravest pity goes out of course for the
"Study in Dejection," that sad affair of the dis-
carded rocking-horse, exposed and neglected by the
door of a secondhand shop. We proceed with quickened sensibilities through a touching speculation on
the descent in the world of this poor beast, till Mr.
Beerbohm turns upon us in the end with a rightabout
frisk of wisdom and wit. Yet what more likely sentimentalist shall we find than he who forever declines
to sever pose from fact?

But that little rocking-horse is real. Our grief for
his fallen fortunes is a nice refraction from the plane
where griefs are all too genuine. And it is this lucky

sight for the essential, this sober value not for effect but for effects, which achieves not only elegance but beauty. The little thing shines out with no parade of impressionism — luminous, deftly fashioned, fresh, done somehow for permanence, whether for mirth or for memorial. So the world we know looks out at us, significant or comfortable: a welcoming drugget of light across an evening road, the pale seaside of winter, the imperceptible promise of a frontier, the racy footing of an antique dance; so we catch the faces of our fellow-folk, a pale boy going back to school or a clergyman who once said " But " to Dr. Johnson. The delightful " Word for Pictures " are always right, — whether they paint a fat god of Hokusai or an abandoned Ariadne making the best of a convenient Bacchus. And there are live sprouts of extemporaneous criticism ungarnered among the litter of " lost columns," like the illumined review of Hardy's *Dynasts*. There are memorable pictures of the noted and ill-spared dead, the inextinguishable youth in Aubrey Beardsley, that unforgettable boy — the old man Swinburne in the " Tupperrossettine " dining-room at Hampstead, the variety of Herbert Beerbohm Tree, vivid Coquelin come unbelievably to dust. Here, clear, firm, fragile, gay, is that transient creature man, a gallant flash in the dark.

" The thing is subtly and therefore truly done," Mr. Beerbohm has said somewhere. There is nothing better to be said for the best of his own, if we are careful still to insist that for him the best subtlety is simple. It is true that his first spoken sentence must have lisped in preciosity. " I write elaborately, for that is my habit," he observes in a humoresque. Nor could we willingly spare his special coinages and special cadences — above all the cadences, for if he did not follow headlong the quest of the *mot juste,* which he has called " the Holy Grail of the nineties," he was merely occupied with the guarded flights and the nice retards of his triumphant little rhythms. His essential ingenuities have made for indolence of effect. " I liked the delusion that I spoke French well," he says somewhere. " Somehow I seemed likely to possess that accomplishment." And with good reason. One is often in his pages reminded of French prose, in that supple touch, light-fingered, neat, — with the characteristic excellence of surface. It is prose cherished by its maker, as prose too seldom is in English, as an art in itself, prose of an English writer who has dared to say in English that for the style's sake he prefers prose to verse, and in prose the essay to the novel or romance.

Serious in style, if nowhere else, he is nevertheless not entirely serious about it. Hence perhaps the especially English quality which calls us back even from our French comparisons — the casualness with which Mr. Beerbohm has declined to make religion of his art. For the long line of English prose-makers, who, now that Matthew Arnold is under partial eclipse, we may venture sometimes to call great, have never regarded themselves, their burden or their style, with the last solemnities. We greet in

Mr. Beerbohm's criticism his special relish for the thing that is " idly done," or in another mood for the value of inexperience " making cerebration compulsory " in style. He is a connoisseur of manner, dandy of the phrase, but he has always found fact more alluring than form. He has admitted, unashamed and unconcerned, " how much more interesting life is than any book or any play."

HENRYK SIENKIEWICZ, 1918

[This essay has been reprinted in its original form as a wartime
memorial.]

I

HENRYK SIENKIEWICZ should have died
when there would have been time for the word
of literary honour. He has gone to his grave with but
a cursory acknowledgment of his eminence in the
world of letters. His genius has represented most
familiarly to the Western world Polish character and
Polish patriotism; but at this acute crisis in Polish
history, individual tribute to that genius dissociate
from its nationalism, has been withheld as an impertinence. Any critical memorial for Sienkiewicz,
if we indulge it at present, must be but the recognition of his service to the " hope of Poland," that
Poland which, in the restrained words of a Sienkiewicz appeal, " has deserved well of humanity."

She has deserved best, by the very preservation
of her hope. For the persistence of the Polish national genius, obstinate through apparent extinction
and reënforced by national tragedy, is the best reassurance we have in these stricken days when men's
hearts fail them for looking after the things which
are coming on the earth. Long ago Sienkiewicz liked

to repeat, for Polish comfort, the old saying of Charneyetski: " I am grown not out of salt nor out of the soil, but out of that which pains me." And today there is international need for such consolation. We watch with misgiving on the battlefields of Europe the visible reality of the old Greek myth, where the children born of the dragon's teeth destroy one another implacably, sorrowfully. Have we always been sure that none can quell the spirit of England? Then why the note of defiance in our chants of love? Shall the spirit of the chainless mind be certainly and eternally French? Yet how often in history the prophecy has been fulfilled: " The time shall come when mighty Ilion shall be laid low! " But in the clutch of doubt we may remember the Polish nation, come to true national consciousness since it lost its place upon the map, wrought into discipline from the necessities of impotence, schooled in development by the pressure of hostile propaganda and expropriation. We may remember too that Polish literature, grown richly self-expressive through national sorrow, which has achieved its characteristic utterances from the inspiration of patriotic shame.

In the scale of this distinguished literature our Western minds should, under no circumstances, venture to fix the place of Sienkiewicz. We are prone, they tell us, to ascribe to him a disproportionate eminence in the lively Polish fiction of the present. We may accept without dispute the qualified applause of those European critics who would temper the excesses of the Sienkiewicz cult and assert that

Sienkiewicz expresses but partially the contemporary spirit, " in its humanitarian inquietude and social fervour." For this very limitation he may represent all the better that body of the new Poland for whom before the War the national question was prior and essential to all others, which was not merely modern or democratic, but doggedly Polish.

He was not of the old Poland nourished upon sacrificial dreams and noble delusions. With his contemporaries he had left far behind the high-strung traditions of the great romantics, their ecstatic devotion to the sheer ideal of Polish rebirth, which made the immortal life of Mickiewicz and Krasinski — their exultations from despair rejected, their tense companionship with passion-charged abstractions, their apocalyptic visions of a " holy Poland," whose sorrows, like unto none other sorrows, should work redemption. Such faith, torture-nourished, was fine even in disease. But the Poland of recent years has not sought to save herself by ideals alone. She has been pitted not against the dominations of evil in abstract places, but against flesh and blood, that is to say against Germany and autocratic Russia. She must persist and increase by methods learned from Germany. And she has had to better the instruction.

Sienkiewicz, then, was of the new Poland which would prefer to walk without fainting rather than to soar with eagles. He was of the Poland which had learned, according to the interpretation of its leaders, to admit economic necessity and geographical *ultimatum*. He was of the strong spirits mobilized for work in that nation of dreamers, who would grapple with oppression by counter-construction and oppose to encroachment the conservation of force, which would strengthen the Polish character for the race struggle by a policy of criticism and deliberate disillusion. Still Sienkiewicz was of the camp which, recognizing the consequence of the practical issue, would still preserve for the Polish struggle the idealism necessary for its success: " I see the necessity for quiet and iron labour, but I do not see the necessity for the repudiation or renunciation of any ideals. And I will tell you too that the Pole who does not bear that great ideal at the bottom of his soul is in a measure a renegade."

II

The share of Sienkiewicz in this common labour was to discover and to liberate in fiction the springs of national health. His was a courageous choice for a subject of Russian Poland, where under the bureaucratic rule, for all the stirrings of potential energy, the faith of reformers must act with least assurance; where the patriot, denied the privilege of efficient service, must see the kernel of society threatened with decay, stricken with civic disease which it was not permitted to cure. In such environment fiction for fiction's sake may well have seemed to Sienkiewicz, as to his fellows, fit only for his aversion, the decadent and the *dilettante*. Still less could he restrain his native abundance within the canon of the problem novel. Why contemplate too steadily problems which it is forbidden to solve? His regenerative service must be a contribution to national fiction, wholesome, sound, and vigorous, " for the strengthening of hearts." " Let us speak," said Bigiel in *Children of the Soil,* " not of death but life, and of that which is best in it, health."

In quest of health and not in romantic rejection of modern reality, Sienkiewicz made the frequent reversions to the past for which he has been reproached.

He has been little prone to salve his country's humiliation by recollection of former glories, by the vainglorious and elegiac retrospect which has enfeebled many a noble Polish energy. To the Polish reformer, he has felt, less than to another is the regretful backward look permitted. He has known — none better — the glamour of arms, the zest for the old-time military skill, and the pride in Polish valour. But he has had little heart to recall the spectacle of a speciously triumphant Poland. The *Knights of the Cross* unrolls to our vision the victorious field of Tannenburg but performs, without passion, its duty of killing and slaying. *On the Field of Glory* achieves its plot before the glory begins. And the masterpiece of the Trilogy prefers to end with the fall of Kamenyets, with the deluge of Turkish invasion barely resisted, relegating to the perfunctory finalities of an epilogue the fame of Hotin and Vienna.

Nor has he looked back, in the characteristic Polish style, to complain at the age-long suffering of that Polish land enriched by the blood of centuries. He shows her in her prolonged distress, oft-shattered breakwater of Europe against oriental devastation, the stamping ground of sweeping hordes, desolated by Cossack vengeance, raided by the perpetual advance and retreat of Europe's preying armies. And the repressed sorrow for that protracted discipline, sorrow as unsentimental as restrained, works at times to utterance more telling for its reticence. So heavily is fulfilled the curse read in the dying eyes of a tortured Cossack, as he watches the Polish legions passing by: " May God punish you, and your children, and your grandchildren to the tenth generation, for the blood, for the wounds, for the torment! God grant that you perish, you and your race, that every misfortune may strike you! God grant that you be continually dying and may never be able either to die or to live! "

Nor has Sienkiewicz looked back primarily to condemn — to ascribe to Poland's improvidence the responsibility for her failure. His corrective criticism he has given, to be sure, with candour and without abatement. Unblinking as history, he has interpreted her suffering as no Messianic sacrifice but as retribution, however heavy, for her own sins. For always the work of Sienkiewicz, from *With Fire and Sword* to *Whirlpools,* presents a frank study of the Polish character. He shows it in its generosities — its gusto and its magnanimity, its capacity for high devotion, its passions sensitive and intense. He reveals with a no less thorough discernment the springs of its weak-

ness — its *penchant* for evasion and self-deception,
its denial of fact, its indolence and its indulgences.
There is the civic irresponsibility of magnates con-
demning in advance to ruin all expended good — the
spectacle of a Vishnyevetski denied the leadership
lest he lead too well, a Voevoda of Vityebsk losing for
a feast a precious military opportunity, a Boguslav
Radzivill pulling, in shameless rivalry with foreign
traitors, for his share of the red cloth, the common-
wealth. There is the turbulent Schlachta stirred to
aimless mutiny or to accidental veto by some chance
Zagloba. There is the instability of a whole people
stampeding from frontier to frontier, following with
equal ease a wind of heroism or a wind of panic. But
Sienkiewicz does not dissect the faults of his countrymen for the love of censure.

Rather with a hope deliberate and daring has he
turned back for the comfort of a faint-hearted present to discover in a past, acknowledged corrupt, the
springs of national energy. Boldly, therefore, he
chose for the epic background of his Trilogy, that
master creation of his prime vigour, *With Fire and
Sword, The Deluge, Pan Michael*, the otherwise dis-
piriting narrative of Poland's seventeenth century,
when the nation was crumbling to patent ruin from
outside attack and interior debasement. But from
these teeming records of violence and treachery, of
nobilities drifting unregarded, of sacrifice bound to
predestined waste, of private virtue deflowered by
public shame, one takes the impress of an energy
wholesome, active, unimpaired. Let the impotent

busy themselves with their dismal moral-mongering!
Let those who lack courage find voice for jeremiads!
"Let us speak not of death but of life, and of that
which is best in it, health!"

The very romance of the Sienkiewicz novel is as
healthy as the wind blowing from the clean steppes.
Here is a stirring land of thrilling change and sweeping chance, apt for Cossack glory and Cossack vengeance, for the hanker of Tarter rapacity or for the
stealing of brides. Here love is fair as from the
foundation of the hills but tipped with danger and
quickened by the zest of hovering tragedy. Here,
too, with a superb literary generalship, are fought
the recurring battles, compelling in their mastery
and their tingle of martial enthusiasm, sufficient for
the beguiling of any pacifist, however conscientious,
if caught off his guard. Let him even once watch
Volodyovski at a duel, and like one of our novelist's
converted priests he will reach for the imaginary
sabre which ought not to be at his side. Here too, we
must own, is a frank brutality in the ungloved han-
dling of horrors, an apparent relish for their description, which passes at times the measure even of historical thoroughness. But brutality Sienkiewicz
would maintain to be far more respectable than the
niceties of fastidious decadence.

III

For the essential art of Sienkiewicz, true to its
principle of health, has created its abundance from

human nature's great simplicities. Distrustful of a society subtilized and world-weary, impatient of mincing refinements, he has sought most willingly, even in studies of artificial environment, those elementary emotions by which all men together rejoice and suffer. They are evident in beauty frank and unconscious where hearts are honest and grown to maturity in clear air. His art at its best is developed by strokes bold and strong. Thus for an early unpretentious work *Charcoal Sketches* was an apt title. And, with few exceptions, in the later plots of ambitious scope the lines are plain, full, broadly suggestive.

First among life's simplicities is pity. And the early short stories, keen with a cosmopolitan diversity which flits from the triflings of the Riviera to the raw American backwoods, are, in significant majority, tales of searching pathos. The finest have always that pathos known best to Sienkiewicz, for all his wanderings, of the peasant soul of the Polish village, honest, stupid, inarticulate, faithful, caught somehow in the trailings of the larger life above and around which it is unable to understand. Such is the quality of the unbearable *Charcoal Sketches*, tragedy of a cottage home wrecked in the stupid village world, where a chance rascal pulls the strings while the intelligent gentry hold aloof. There is little Yanko too, the musician, weak thread of life in an abortive body, slighted, disregarded, broken to death, but a soul of exquisite harmony, and withal a helpless child. Always the demand upon our tenderness is direct, even obvious, but at best compelling, humane with the common knowledge of the common grief.

Here is laughter too, hearty and ungrudging, breath of a strong spirit in a strong body. It is the unquenchable utterance of that interior humour, in which critics have felt Polish literature deficient. Wit there is too in plenty, if we can stop to note that by-product, always with Sienkiewicz easily superior, in its intimate sagacity and off-hand vigour, to the *bon mot* of the professional amateur. But most considerable contribution of Sienkiewicz to the fibre of Polish literature is his distinctive humour, creative rather than critical, broad rather than subtle. It is the unwearied relish for the simple traits of human nature freshly discovered with surprise, ever fresh in the recognition of their truth. Whoso has followed the huddling thoughts of Polanyetski dressing for his wedding, has heard the antiphonal drunkenness of the Bukoyemskis, or has seen the cowardice of Zagloba transformed by fright to sudden valour, has witnessed a spontaneous humour, free play of organic exuberance, rising by natural necessity like a clean fire in pure air.

Here is love too in open frankness, a primary force. We may study, if we will, its debasement in the toyings of a corrupt Warsaw, degraded to a game of sentiment, wantonness, and truant passion. We may watch it in *Without Dogma,* the expense of a palsied spirit in a waste of shame. We may trace in *Children of the Soil* its slow education in the bond of marriage. But its characteristic appearance is in the energy of a fresh and strong-blooded youth, where passion and devotion are surging together in a robust mixture of reverence and clean animalism, frankly physical, but offensive only to the squeamish as the sign not of indulgence but of fecundity.

Here is the religious instinct. For the typical Pole has still in his heart, we may suspect, some Chensto-hova, shrine neglected or belittled, but at the threat of hostile defacement a rallying place for high devotion. Sienkiewicz, to be sure, has written as the partisan for whom defence of Catholicism is something more pleasant to him still — the best anti-Russian propaganda. He has written besides as the assured reformer. Knowledge alone could be potent enough to save his Poland. And in the thought even of his atheist, Swidwicki, " Knowledge without religion breeds only thieves and bandits." But there is more than intelligent policy in the revelation of that Catholic worship shown rarely beautiful in souls genuine and kindly — the priest Kordetski whose faith once removed more than mountains in the Polish cause, the naïf and strong-souled cavaliers of old time whose trust undoubting was a breastplate and a handy weapon. It is revealed most fair in the hearts of good women in days new or old. It rests serene and stable, amid the modern drift of belief and unbelief, waiting for the moment of large experience to alter life's proportions and to recall, within the modern soul, the elementary need to bow down — an end to which, by the suggestion of Sien-

kiewicz well versed in skepticisms, all flesh shall
come. " Destruction takes all philosophies and systems, one after another, but Mass is said as of old."

Here too is the love of the soil, instinct rudimen-
tary and universal, essential to the sound life of the
Polish character, homely comfort of the Polish heart.
It is an instinct as natural as the return of the mole
to his little burrow. Hence the dumb tragedy of up-
rooted life at each upheaval of a peasant home.
Hence the tenacity instructed and reënforced, which
has magnified beyond calculation the life and death
grapple for the soil of Posen against illegal expropriation. Each social theory must be, in the opinion of
Sienkiewicz, partial or untenable, which regards the
land only as an economic factor, and not as the root
of a profound affection. In this affection for the
" holy land " is the life of sober security, temperate,
wholesome, close to the ground, busy with the primordial labour, in company with the very processes
of growth. " That," says the Marynia of Polanyetski, " is the real work on which the world stands,
and every other is either the continuation of it or
something artificial. . . . In all other relations that
a man holds there may be deceit, but the land is
truth." And the search of the Polanyetski family
for the full endowment of normal living takes them
back at last to the country estate to become " children of the soil."

The sights and sounds of that Polish land so often
desolate are never far from our direct vision in
the pages of Sienkiewicz. There are the fields fertile

and grain-laden, the lines of alders beyond the
meadow stretches, the ponds golden in the evening
sun, the mists rising under the stars, the nightingale
and the homelike frog, the cheerful surroundings of
quiet husbandry dependent, as of old, upon the harvest. From such remembrance, Sienkiewicz, ac-
quainted with wandering, has given his share to the
literature of the Polish exile. For, from the lodgings
of the Polish dispersion has come perhaps the world's
most wistful poetry of home; and from the waters
of their many Babylons the Poles have perhaps most
tenderly remembered Sion. Sienkiewicz, intimate
with the dumb suffering of the peasant heart, has
told in *After Bread,* with compassionate understanding, the story of the yearning emigrant, helpless alike
before treachery of agents, the misguided efforts of
eager benevolence, his own bewilderment, and the
relentless mechanism of the strong Western world.
A pure image of the homesick soul is the lighthouse
keeper of Aspinwall, weary of heart, leaf-tossed to a
rest at last, who is beguiled from his post by a Polish
book and the words of Mickiewicz dearest to the
exile: " Litva, my country, thou art health! "

But the cherished soil is but the substance of the
thing unseen, the country of the patriot's devotion.
For her sake good men and true are content with
barren sacrifice and unacknowledged labour. Cleav-
ing to her and to the receding hope of her public
good, they leave father, brother, wife. Her sins at
least can be seventy times seven forgiven. Her in-
gratitude, if hers alone, can be endured with pardon

and serenity. Theirs is a common desire — their mother " Poland as they wish her to be." Theirs is a common discipline — the preference of the common service to their personal and immediate ambitions.

IV

These who yearn and pray and laugh and love are folk of a sinewy stock, with coursing blood and a tactile sense of muscle and bone, emanating vigour and life. Sienkiewicz, however liable to critical rigours on the score of taste or tolerance, is easily superior as the creator. Taught by experience vivid and humane, trained in an apprenticeship of labour unstinted, able by nature to catch character in the act, he built up the power for the making of men. His production of later years flagged, to be sure, the execution grown mechanical, the exuberance slackened. But in the best work of Sienkiewicz, the virile product of his first maturity, as seldom in fiction, the word has been made flesh.

For our surest estimate as for our first delight we turn still, as of course, to the Trilogy, where the creative power, educated in the school of the short story, was first let loose for its ambition, the mastery of life in big units upon a background of epic scope.

From the crowd of faces fierce and strongly set, stamped with the marks of force or of ferocity, rise to distinctness the dignitaries of the historical background. They bear illustrious names of forgotten lustre, come alive again from the old muster rolls, each apprehended in his life-motive, good or ignoble. Some few, like the idealized Sobieski, are touched up with a romantic glamour to suit the heroics of the story. But for the most part they are big and plainly natural, thrust into a clearness just yet merciful. There is the traitor Lyubormirski, drawn to honourable duty by an appeal with which flattery is shrewdly mixed, but capable of the betrayal to which he is destined by his nature and by the temptations of the time. There is the lord of Zamost in his fortress, self-satisfied, unalterably complacent. There is the wreck of the noble Radzivill, folding in upon himself the dark tragedy of his lonely treachery and crumbling ambition.

But the immortal figures of the Sienkiewicz Trilogy are not oppressively eminent. They are our friends familiar and dear through the long companionship of the woven story, strongly, simply revealed. We know them the better that their traits are few. There is little Volodyovski, of insignificant figure but most significant sabre, simple soldier, simple lover, simple soul. There is his Basia, vivid, valorous, dauntless as a young Tartar. There is Jendzian, rosy and sleek servant, insinuating profit and suggesting reward, faithful even to perfidy for the sake of his master alone. There is the headlong Kmita, most winning of all the young fire-eaters dear to Sienkiewicz, incredibly daring, incredibly devoted, " knowing not how to love or how to hate with half a heart."

And there is Zagloba, acknowledged master-creature of Sienkiewicz, most lovable of blusterers, better at drinking than Sir Toby Belch, more inventive of brags than Falstaff. The comparison with Falstaff is as inevitable as it has become conventional. For these two are together. But Sienkiewicz has perhaps claimed justly for Zagloba an even better right to the respect and affections of men. In his company, however, we are not fastidious for virtues. We love him as he reprehensively is — boastful, gloriously mendacious, fertile in lies which hurry to mind so fast that he cannot always choose among them, which grow in geometrical progression with time and with his audience — wise in stratagem, valiant in extremity, companionable, with his humour not over nice but as ready as breath, clearest under the stimulus of fright. We love him best, to be sure, in his faithful if sudden heroisms, in his devoted friendships, in his inimitable understanding of human weakness and human truth. It is a sorrow to leave him at the last with the tongue grown quiet forever, cowering in broken age by the coffin of Volodyovski, convinced at last that he is old. Far more easily can we bear the ultimate humiliation of Falstaff, babbling of green fields and thinking upon God. Sienkiewicz dealt relentlessly by his Trilogy to quench its spirits at the end. For whether our good friends of these pages are dead or forever out of sight we take our everlasting farewell of them with a sharp protest of personal loss. We have had " an old custom to have them in our fellowship."

v

The superb vigour of the Sienkiewicz historical Trilogy has drawn to itself a stress of appreciation, slighting perhaps to the remarkable modern studies. Though he has chosen for his characteristic material the genuine stuff of large simplicities, he has possessed a lively share of the Polish *penchant* for analysis. He has known how to attack with relish and comprehension the contemporary types of urban ineptitude. He has portrayed, with protest but with masterly understanding, the *coterie* of " artists without portfolios," the Bukovski of *Children of the Soil,* collector and connoisseur, who, having dallied away his gifts, comes one day to die, " having eaten bread and not paid for it "; the Sidwicki of *Whirlpools,* cynic who defiles with venom the society upon which he lives; Ploszowski of *Without Dogma,* who deadens the capacity of a gifted spirit by the drug of introspection.

But even these scenes of futile eddy are but the setting for the Sienkiewicz theme of health. Within the vapid trifling of lives desultory or unclean stands always among types of lesser beauty one nature pure and regenerative, one true soul loving and sincere, which, carrying in itself the principle of growth, remains potent to cleanse. It is, by the usual message of Sienkiewicz, the eternal soul of woman, created joyous and clean of heart from nature's abundant fountains, chastened to understanding power by experience sweetly received. She is called Marynia in

Children of the Soil, Aniela in *Without Dogma.* She is the Hanka of *Whirlpools,* the only spot of unconquered beauty in that desert of drifting sands.

Sound study of contemporary Polish society could not shirk the political issue. Treatment of the theme by Sienkiewicz, a Russian subject of the old *régime,* needed caution and reserve, tempered by the patience which intellectual captivity has taught the Poles. But the criticism, when it has appeared, has been all the more telling that it has not usurped the novelist's consciousness to the loss of art's essential sanity.

Sienkiewicz has not wasted strength in unapplied hatred of his enemies. Still less has he adopted the " romantic " policy of loving them. He did not wait for modern political criticism to identify the German as the natural enemy of the Pole. From his early work, he set forth with hostile candour that stern and respectful animosity for the German which is the most deeply rooted of Polish instincts. *The Diary of a Tutor of Poznan* traces with even uncharacteristic vehemence, and less than characteristic humour the tragedy of a delicate Polish boy suffering in the German schools from the handicap of the unfamiliar language and the deliberate indignities of the German discipline. *The Knights of the Cross,* that sombre narrative of brutal, half-pagan days, has a theme selected, not first by Sienkiewicz in Polish letters, for the chance it offers to flog the Germans over the shoulders of the Teutonic Knights. And *Bartek the Victor,* unbearable tragedy of the Posen conscription for the Franco-Prussian war, casts more pitiful enlightenment upon the blind cruelty of to-day's unwilling mobilizations for service in a conqueror's army than a dozen reports of Polish commissions.

Of Russian Poland under Tsarism, seething vortex of opposing theories and restive discontents, Sienkiewicz gave at last a political study sufficiently telling in his bleak and sorrowful *Whirlpools*. The narrative of modern revolutionary confusions, tentative, lawless, ineffectual, is rather a manifesto than a novel. Here, for once in the Sienkiewicz mould, fiction is stiffened to symbolism, by an analysis so thorough and so sombre as to seem at times the finish of disillusion. It raises a voice of warning weighted with prophecy, lifted in a wilderness of drifting wastes. It is known for the authentic voice of Sienkiewicz by its bold grasp of a complete civic condition; by its sagacity keen but unyielding, by the consistent set of a temperament conservative for all its liberality, hostile to disorder; by its solemn and insistent summons to the preservation of the national hope as the superlative and single duty.

Disdain for the inferior Russian bureaucracy, implicit in the very silences of Sienkiewicz, despite his rally-cry to Russian colours at the opening of the War, is in this book sufficiently patent. This is " the race which does not know how to live and does not permit anybody else to live." Theirs is the official-dom venal, retrogressive, stupidity rigorous, which ties the hands of the generous and law-abiding, leaving banditry and anarchy at large. Theirs is the galling check upon popular enlightenment through which alone the country is to see salvation.

Nor are the Poles exempt from the arraignment. Through the eyes of Gronski, type of a culture patriotic, liberal, but helpless, we watch the frittering of factional energy in the folly of counter-agitation. There are the National Democrats, interpreted, as we should expect from the pen of Sienkiewicz, as a force organized, patriotic, liberal, consistent, but thwarted in effectual propaganda by the tamperings of irresponsible opposition. There are the Conservatives favourable to the Russian *entente*, sensible, adroit, but short-sighted for far horizons, ready like Esau to relinquish an ultimate heritage for an immediate paltry benefit. " And with us it is not permitted to relinquish anything."

There is the *bête noir* of Sienkiewicz, the Polish Socialist party, blamed for the sporadic violence of its desultory revolutionism, assailed in its logic as " national-cosmopolitan," derided for its Russian affiliations. But the primary attack accords with the dogma of the stout nationalist: that the struggle for the national existence, risked and enfeebled by the struggle of classes, was essential even to economic reform. " Our Socialists have undertaken the construction of a new house, forgetting that we live huddled together in a few rooms, and that in the others dwell strangers who will not assent to it; or rather on the contrary they will permit the demolition of those few rooms, but will not allow their reconstruction."

Whatever the policy or theory under test, we have

but the spectacle of effort expended in vain. In vain the wary reforms of benevolent landowners. In vain the choice evolution of superior culture, destroyed like the fine flower Marynia, in a moment of unmotived violence. A heavier condemnation still is implied in the moral failure of the youthful Kryzcki, type of the kindly and progressive noble, proved unequal to the finest test of discipline and self-control. " Neither love for woman nor for fatherland will suffice. He will love them, and in a given case will perish for them. But in life he will indulge himself." So ends, by a stern verdict, the ancient leadership of the Polish noble: " Such as he will not rebuild society."

Before revelations so inexorable and so unpleasant it seems at times as if Sienkiewicz, in his later years, accepted for himself the conclusion of his cynic Swidwicki: " With us there are only whirlpools. And these not whirlpools upon a watery gulf beneath which is a calm depth, but whirlpools of sand. And the sterile sand buries our traditions, our civilization, our culture, our whole Poland, and transforms her into a wilderness upon which flowers perish and only jackals can live." But the true Sienkiewicz answers in the person of the irrepressible optimist Szremski: " Beneath these whirlpools which are whirling upon the surface of our life there is something which Swidwicki did not perceive. There is a bottomless depth of suffering. . . . With us the people awake in the morning and follow the plow in the field, go to the factory, to the offices, behind the

benches in the shops, and all manner of labour — in
pain. And why do we suffer thus? . . . It would be
sufficient for everyone to say to Her, this Poland of
whom Swidwicki says that she is perishing, ' Too
much dost Thou vex me; therefore I renounce Thee,
and from this day wish to forget Thee! And nobody
says that. . . . Jackals seek carrion, not suffering.
. . . So she lives in everyone of us, in all of us together, and will survive all the whirlpools in the
world. And we will set our teeth, and will continue
to suffer for Thee, Mother, and we, and if God wills
it so — our children and our grandchildren, will renounce neither Thee nor hope."

VI

Perhaps the unsentimental Zagloba would command to " make boots for dogs of such consolation."
And, indeed, the optimism of Sienkiewicz persisted
upon a more palpable basis than this restrained survival of the old Messianic dedication. The policies
may have failed in the nation of politicians; the no-
bles, ancient staple of Polish stock, may have lapsed
from prestige. " There remains yet the solid multitude of country peasants. Formerly Dobrowski's
March was a watchword for a hundred thousand; today it is a watchword for ten million." And in Hanka
Skibianka, peasant woman chanced upon culture, is
incarnate that which was, before the mortalities of
the Great War, a hope sufficiently tangible for democratic Poland. She moves across the dark pages in a

bright beauty able to heal and to revive, a figure of power, radiating health, strong to carry, brave to defend, young to endure, " with a heart of a Polish village simple and faithful." She will achieve her honour at the cost of sorrow; she will exact the reverence due to her full womanhood; and when men think of her, they roll up their sleeves for work.

By the preservation of such optimism, sustained however saddened, Sienkiewicz achieved the supreme contribution of his genius to Polish energy. By the indomitable spirit of his lifetime's work, he sufficiently vindicated the inherent vitality of Polish culture. For it is the optimism of unconditioned vigour conscious of its function.

" Because I come of a society in which so much power is wasted," he wrote in an early essay, " every planned and completed work fills me with real respect, and has for me also some wonderful and exceptional charm. Whenever I write *Finis,* at the close of a book of mine, I feel something like a sensation of delight not only because the labour is done, but because of the sensation which comes of a finished work. . . . A whole series of books, especially when written in the name of a leading idea, is a life task accomplished; it is a harvest home festival in which the leader of the workmen has earned the right to a garland and a song, ' I bring fruit! I bring fruit! ' "

And in this assumption of power and production, easily accorded to the distinguished dead, is still a strong promise for the hope of Poland. For we may accept for our " lucky word " at the grave of Sienkiewicz the prophecy, however qualified, of George Brandes, no great lover of Sienkiewicz, but a good lover of Poland: " The future is not to the avenger, nor," altogether, alas, " to the apostle, but to him who labours with genius."

VII

SIR THOMAS BROWNE AGAIN

I

SIR THOMAS BROWNE is apparently one of the few literary themes that never go quite out of style. Whoso would dust the tombs of most seventeenth century worthies, delightful as they usually are, must pretend to find a controversial opening and address himself to scholars. But essays on Sir Thomas Browne recur like the cycles of the seasons and for the most part with as little apology. Perhaps the secret is that we write as often as not for the appetite of youth. And for youth the discovery of old Sir Thomas still preserves its special zest.

I fancy that the sprouting self-consciousness of youth sees in the *Religio Medici* something of its own likeness. For honest egotism, interested and interesting, never tires of its common theme, which is of eternity where " there is no distinction of tenses," — well enough stated in the oft-quoted utterance of a modern arch-egoist: " I dote on myself — There is that lot of me and all so luscious." But the egotism of Sir Thomas Browne is generous and genial, never assertive or bumptious. It is the pleasure in its own processes of a curious spirit, born and trained to take

notice, finding everywhere a stimulus to suggestion
or a subject for speculation philosophical or " paradoxical." And always at hand is the delectable material, himself. " It is a poor center of a man — himself," Bacon might say when he chanced to have on
the garment of morality. But it is a good center —
none better — for literary revelation. And Sir
Thomas was justified by centuries of Renaissance
tradition that lay behind him.

By his time the anonymous self-effacement of the
Middle Ages had long been past. They were in full
swing still when Chaucer paid his visit to Lady Fame
and was asked if he came to beg notoriety: " Nay,"
says Chaucer,

> " I cam not hither, graunt mercy,
>   For none swich cause, by mine hed.
> Suffice me, if I be ded,
>   That no wight han my name in honde."

But at nearly the same time the fashion to talk
personalities down the ages was frankly set by Pe-
trarch's letter to Posterity and his candid assumption that Posterity would care to know with somewhat ample comprehensiveness what manner of man
he was.

Browne's seventeenth century ambition has in it a
more modest working. I doubt if he reckons at all
upon his repute with coming generations. He lives
in an age of more tempered self-assertion, besides,
of smaller people. Here is no superabundance of
quality as in the tonic outrageosities of a Rabelais

or the diverse humanities of a Montaigne. Avidity
for fame is here superseded just by an engaging
penchant for confidential reverie. Renaissance Ti-
tanism has given place to self-differentiation. Personality has already achieved its heights. It has perhaps sounded its depths. But its details and its
specialties are inexhaustible. And why search, like
Burton, in his *Anatomy of Melancholy* the repositories of pathological gossip, for odds and ends, prin-
cipally odds, of character, when each man has
within himself the most accessible laboratory and
most entertaining material for observation? Browne
besides is not an anatomy of melancholy, but a
healthy, and, as he suggests, an uncommonly favourable specimen — very special indeed, except in the
concern of his sins, which are " not singular but epi-
demical." So he will " difference himself nearer and
draw into a lesser circle."

II

We accept with least qualification, perhaps, among
the claims of Browne to singularity, his equable and
stable tolerance. Few in his age could sustain themselves by any sort of spiritual levitation above the
thick of controversy. More had achieved it as an
ideal for Utopia at least. But it was a quaint thing
still in the seventeenth century to find a thinker who
could admit freely the possibility that he might be
mistaken, who could suspect that there are " not
many controversies worth a passion," who could not

" conceive why a difference in opinion should divide an affection."

Browne does not naturally want to kill a snake, nor does he shrink from a Frenchman. Stout Anglican as he is, he has no aggressive antipathy which constrains him to insult a Catholic. He can acknowledge his duty to use good language toward the Pope and to " withhold the title of Antichrist." At sight of a procession with a crucifix he can " dispense with his hat more easily than with the thought of his Maker." He can write the following imaginative sentence: " I could never divide myself from any man upon the difference of an opinion, or be angry with his judgment for not agreeing with me in that from which within a few days I should dissent myself." The suggestion of complacence here hinders very little the note of urbane good-fellowship.

Liberality has its reward in a gift for canny and pertinent reflection. Here is a judgment sound and shrewd, at once elevated and sane, quickly responsive to significance. Hence appear amid the intricacies wrought by Browne's somewhat oblique intelligence, clear patches of illumined wisdom or glorified common sense. He has the sufficiently clear sight. So he is able for all his speculation to avoid blind alleys of idiosyncracy in thought: " Those have not only depraved understandings but diseased affections which cannot enjoy a singularity without an Heresie, or be author of an opinion without they be that of a sect also."

Very engagingly, however, Browne confesses his

oddities of thought or of temper. There is his unaccountable dread of death for all his professional familiarity therewith. He can avow himself frankly "as wholesome a morsel for the worms as any." He can state blithely his preference for cremation, to go to corruption " the neatest way." There remains that recoil, not from the fearfulness of death but from the shame of it. Less comprehensible even in a physician seems his unscientific scorn for the processes of human generation, the " trivial and vulgar " way for the perpetuation of the race. But we recognize as quite appropriate and natural the consistent whimsy of Browne, the set of his fancy toward the queer and unfamiliar. There is the difficult phrase far fetched from the chambers of his imagery. There is the taste for delectable marvels of superstition, even though as in *Vulgar Errors* they are ostensibly introduced to be refuted: pleasant problems as to whether there be griffins in nature, whether the chameleon lives only on air, whether the elephant hath joints. There is the more scholarly drawing toward the oddities of archaeology, to curiosities of ancient wisdom and speculation. Hence the relish of the *Hydriotaphia* for mortuary relics, the riot of hieroglyphical figures, the zest for "Homeric urns " and " sepulchral treasures," for " ossuaries " whose persons have " entered the famous nations of the dead." In the *Hydriotaphia* Browne shows himself a lover whether or not a scholar of the recondite.

In his treasuring of the suggestive and the enigmatical for its own sake lies perhaps the explanation for the strong flavour of medievalism which obscures our judgment in any attempt to gauge the naturalistic attitude of Browne. He has still a strong clinging to the allegory and riddle of nature. " The severe schools shall never laugh me out of the philosophy of Hermes, that this visible world is but a picture of the invisible." Evidently something of a mathematician, he is possessed by the mystery of numbers and forms; and the symbolism, apt and explicit, of an imaginative geometry is ever ready at hand to his genius for analogy. " I have often admired the mystical ways of Pythagoras and the secret magick of numbers." God is " a skillful geometrician." The characteristic imagery in Browne's style concerns the circle, the right line, the triangle, and the square. And the conception of a quincunctial universe in the *Garden of Cyrus* comes from the same order of thought as the pentangle on the shield of Sir Gawaine.

III

But Browne would tell us of deeper mysteries. Such occult speculations as these are but the inventions of metaphysical fancy. The intrinsic quality of Browne's mind, the essential content of Browne's reverie, concern the unimaginable relations of man with his unimaginable universe. The characteristic quotation from Browne will always remain: " I love to lose myself in a mystery, to pursue my reason to an, O altitudo! "

There is the mystery of death, " eloquent, just and

mighty," theme to which all flesh returns. Seldom has it been realized with more majesty than in the solemn visionary way of seventeenth century meditation; but the *Hydriotaphia* is the special opportunity of Browne. To be sure, he has more concern than we with relics found in tombs or with diverse rituals of burial. He applies a fresher imagination than we can furnish forth to the oldest of moral themes, the vanity of human wishes, the immemorial ironies of death. But in the moulded periods of the noble prose, in the rise and fall of the appropriate cadence, the more poetic concentration here and there of the imagery, we know that Browne has forgotten the antiquary and the moralist in the wonder most ancient of days at the eternal mutability of life: " Behold I tell you a mystery! "

And it is after all for the sake of that dignity in human nature which is inexplicable that Browne returns so surely to the contemplation of personality. He does not, as does Bacon, catch exalted vision of a potential achievement for man in the understanding and use of nature. Unlike Bacon, he would have been shocked by a modern effort at blasphemy: " Glory to man in the highest! " Nor does he find the mind of man interesting for what it can know, — rather because it cannot be known. For therein lies its reach toward God: " There is surely a piece of divinity in us, something that was before the elements, and owes no homage unto the sun."

Nature, too, he would say, is alluring to curiosity not for what may be known of it, but for what may not be known. For this reason, we may venture to say that Browne is not, in the strict use of the term, a philosopher at heart. His mind plays with philosophical problems somewhat as riddles, loving the " paradoxical " therein. It nibbles at the relations of mind and body, hovers in pleasing suppositions about the absolute existence of forms, assumes, with satisfaction at the oddity of the notion, his own existence in the idea of God before creation: " Thus I was dead before I was alive; though my grave be England, my dying place was Paradise; and Eve miscarried of me before she conceived of Cain." But these are only piquant excursions from the main track of his reverie. He who loves a mystery is not a philosopher, — only he who would fain solve it. As for Browne, he is " content to understand a mystery without a rigid definition in an easy and Platonic description." " 'Tis good to sit down with a description, periphrasis, or adumbration. For by acquainting our reason how unable it is to display the visible and obvious effects of nature, it becomes more humble and submissive unto the subtleties of faith." The humble mind is perhaps not the typically philosophical mind. " To believe only possibilities is not faith but mere philosophy."

A sort of religious reverie is therefore the natural field of Browne. Hence his joyful acceptance of all " impossibilities in religion," " not enough for an active faith." To accept the great essentials of Christian theology as the ages have formulated them is to Browne not only an act of willing faith but a positive relief. He gladly leaves to the theologians their responsibility for " the winged mysteries of Divinity," delighting in his freedom to enjoy their subtleties and his own curiosity therewith. To pose his "apprehension with those involved Ænigmas and riddles of the Trinity, the Incarnation, the Resurrection," doctrines wholly accepted by his belief, is to him not an agony, nor a polemical exercise, but " a solitary recreation."

So it is hard to understand the interpretation of critics who find in Sir Thomas Browne a mystic. His pages reveal the temperament of a good and pious man, " of settled years and Christian constitution," courteous beyond parallel toward minds of other faith, courteous, we might say, toward his God, — who apparently, as he says, " conquers sturdy doubts and boisterous objections upon his knees. But he never, we suspect, for all his talk of the experience, quite loses himself like the veritable mystic in his mystery. He enjoys himself far too much to lose himself for a moment. The true mystic will not, we imagine, reach his " O altitudo! " by way of his reason. He will in his belief transcend his reason, and turn himself at last in silence, as Dante bids, " toward the celestial fountains." Essential contemplation is neither amateur speculation, however intelligent, nor spiritual recreation. And Browne is incorrigibly fond of both.

Deliverance from self-differentiation, the dream of the penitent and the mystic alike, would be the denial of his nature. His conclusion for the *Hydrio-*

taphia where he anticipates the adventure of immortality, is a good revelation alike of his quality and of its limitation: " 'Tis all one to lie in St. Innocent's churchyard as in the sands of Egypt, ready to be anything in the exstacy of being ever." He would call " man's chief aim " — to pervert the old phrase of the catechism " to glorify God and to enjoy himself forever."

VIII

A VICTORIAN AT BAY

I

WHEN he happens to observe that some good old Victorian was born a hundred years ago, the wistfulness of the loyal critic stiffens to a resolute confession of faith. Here has come to be the accredited chance for respectful return to the maligned old worthies born in the early decades of the eighteenhundreds, when everybody may renew, unashamed, the pleasant friendships without pretending for the look of the thing to scorn them.

There is saving grace in a century, we have always felt. Once in a hundred years enchanted villages rise from depths of earth to the light; for a hundred years a sleeping princess must repose before the kiss of the marrying prince. We should be perversely blind to analogy if after a hundred years we failed to peer among the dusty litter of " olde bokes." For where is magic more likely to be? We may cease to toe the mark of the current literary issue and remember at leisure with the complacence of recognition the cherished things which we are in the habit of knowing. Yes, let us encourage the world's growing leniency, which permits us to be antiquated if only we will be antiquated enough and allows an old subject to be tolerable if only it be old a century.

For even the most anxious modernist is at home in his own library inconsistently old-fashioned. Whatever his precautions and inoculations, he is constitutionally liable to some kindly predilection for whatever he has once loved. And there is involved in everybody's refusal to forget a former taste only a decent loyalty, just as Sir Roger de Coverley never changed the cut of his clothes after his memorable affair with the Widow. These things once entered our experience with favour, and we owe them more than the " lucky word " meet for the salutation of tombs, — rather the living greeting for a living friend on a sociable birthday feast.

We are advisedly reluctant to disturb with too critical invasion certain good old lanes of romance. Revisited, they seem often homeless and inhuman ways. At least the rumble and racket of lordly words is no longer a charmed incantation. There used to be a great line of Tennyson's:

" Hear, Icenian, Catieuclanian! Hear, Corita-
nian, Trinobant! "

Just who these high beings were I have always dreaded to learn, lest the spell should break. But now I care not for them. I would just as lief hear about Goody Blake and Harry Gill and George and Sarah Green. Day now dawns on Norham's castled steep unheeded, and the curses of Brian the Hermit bring no answering shudder to the blood.

There is always the chance that we may honestly find shrunken some favourite bit of the old world that used to loom so large with the largeness of discovery. For other things than years have lost size since the time-machine began to quicken its revolving pace. " He that hath never seen a river, the first he seeth he taketh it to be an ocean." We have to be careful of our oceans nowadays lest they should turn out to be only five.

With some such faint-hearted scruple the public long held back, lagging, from reunion with the elder novelists. What if those gentle and agreeable young ladies should really be unable to bleed after a good pricking? What if the grand hurly-burly of clamorous excitement should no longer rush us forward, pale and tense, to know the worst? And we depose to a growing fastidiousness in laughter; at least we like our subtlety to be taken for granted. We no longer fancy the quintain type of humour. What if some jovial old comrade should have grown to look amazingly like a clown? What if the caricatures should strain at their insistence so that we " could not miss 'em " ? And we refuse to cry upon compulsion. We no longer linger spell-bound by the death-beds of little Pauls and little Nells. It would be a pity if the laugh should ring with more mirth than it is master of, if the tear should drop bigger than the molecular composition of a tear allows.

There was equal uneasiness about poetry of the Victorians. For in these fields too the critics have been busy with their buckets of cold water, with their chemicals for de-gilding the lily, suggesting furthermore that " the gleam that never was " actually never was at all upon the poets born a hundred years ago.

Where indeed are the poetesses of yesteryear? Their gentleness, their melody, their vehemence, their tenderness, were good, but they are gone or remembered only in condescension. For our early *Sturm und Drang* " the poets of doubt " found the language and release. Should we of today find the doubt too easy, too sheltered in its anguish, for the present chaos? For our first vision of revealed beauty " the poets of art " found the right design, the authentic throb at beauty's pain. Should we find the beauty wilted or overblown, or the fleshliness of the once naughty fleshly school possibly not fleshly enough? Tennyson, who taught us poetry, soon lost the sanction of his priesthood, condemned of sentiment and of prettiness, blighted more than any of his considerable contemporaries by that undetermined poison gas that worked vaguely in the fog, Victorianism. And Browning and his " stuff for strength " ? Who any longer asks us at the luncheon table if we are fond of Browning?

II

But we need not have been afraid. We might have trusted something to our own expanding good-nature and the natural liberality of mature sight for prose or verse.

The free-handed old novelists with whose memory late decades have been busy, knew a potency real enough to outweigh more faults than we shall ever have wit to find. Yes, a hundred years ago, more or less, let us boldly affirm, was a promising time to come into the world, and if the scale of the century has anything to do with endowment, we may have every confidence in the babies of the present. At least for the fellowship of letters Stevenson was right that:

" The dearest friends are the oldest friends,
   And the new are just on trial."

To distrust Dickens, for instance, was surely the cowardice of little faith. We returned to him as to a lost play-fellow. Today we are wiser than we were a little while ago to know what strength is worth — that robust sympathy so much warmer than good taste that excess matters little, spirits so buoyant that their maintenance in this tired world is an exalted service, the easy control of his seething world whose vulgarity no longer shocks our hardened public, the sustained vitality of the definite and lighted vision. We have learned a value for his clear lines; we have ceased parrot-wise, to malign the swift and electric style once held, on hearsay, coarse. And we understand why Thackeray, who saw an immense deal wrong in Dickens, nevertheless willed to praise the work of his more copious and more popular rival, — why he found him " how much the best of all."

To Thackeray himself we grew happily closer in

the freedom of reminiscence, thanks to the welcome excuse which the centenary gave for the release of biographical material despite Thackeray's modest prohibition. The personal Thackeray, kindly man of the world, touched us almost with the charm of a new acquaintance — the grown-up boy who could never see a boy without wanting to give him a sovereign, the chivalrous editor, unparalleled today, who withdrew from the management of the *Cornhill Magazine* because he could not bear to reject the manuscripts of women contributors. And in the novelist, keen but humane, we looked in vain for the cynic who had the elfish trick of spoiling a story, who chose in cold blood to turn out a novel without a hero, who preferred a Lady Castlewood unreasonable, inconsistent, and jealous, a silly Amelia, an irresponsible Pendennis, — when they might more easily have been capital specimens of their kind. We acknowledged with more instructed respect the artist Thackeray, whatever his engaging makeshifts, the artist strong and light of touch, masterly in the even level of his style, moderate of effect, with the sufficient tact of genius which has no need of emphasis or of trick vocabulary. We acknowledged too the realist, wise early in his generation, despite his generation's sentiment, with the courage of disillusion. Him we had almost missed in the earlier days.

And poetry has been safe, however negligent the tides of fashion. Youth's perpetual discovery will not let it wither, nor will the honest opportunism of research stale it. For the centenary has been the chance

not only of the sentimentalist but of the scholar.
The scholar, to be sure, has risked enthusiasm only
with careful precaution. It would certainly not look
well to be caught mistaking a river for an ocean. He
has advanced his mild praises, looking anxiously in
all directions first. His concessions have usually been
characteristic of the " liberal thinker," who, as Newman, that most astute Victorian, would say again,
" never advances a truth without guarding himself
against being supposed to exclude the contradictory."
But even buckets of cold water are often the very
best things for the fields. Centenary biographies and
centenary studies, though prepared with resolute disillusion, may bring their unexpected gifts; for the
real things, as Erasmus told us centuries ago, can
never suffer by being understood. With poets the
centenaries have come too soon perhaps for sound
appraisal or for the foundation of serene cults. They
have not been out of style quite long enough to have
come in again. And some, perhaps, will see but a perfunctory resurrection. For the poetesses, considered
as -esses, let them pass with our kind thanks, to join
the " lady novelists," and to be followed when time
is ripe by the " women voters." Some good chances
for deserved festival we have almost missed, with
Coventry Patmore, with Sydney Dobell. But most
have entered with their hundredth birthday upon
the beginning of a new criticism, for the most part
lucid and instructed, and however timid with praise,
meant for preservation and not for disparagement.

The old poets have been discerned growing in their

generation but have been planted afresh for a new life under a later air. Arnold, noble poet contemplative, may be known for a manlier spirit since even one centenary critic has noted in his neglected social essays a modernness apt for present emergencies. Rossetti of the clear young vision and even of the later more questionable richness, is rescued not only in the fine last word of Sir Edmund Gosse from disrepute. Tennyson is remembered as master of a " style " so large and luminous that he may easily be forgiven for the " manner." And the poetic acclamation some years ago on the hundredth birthday of Browning was best proof of his vitality among those who know best what poetry is and what becomes of it. What though he be no longer table-conversation?

His ancient vogue, which grew with the slowness of the higher organism to maturity, became an inherent part of poetic life, too far below the surface to be disturbed by the flux. His " stuff for strength," plenteous within the most heady and protuberant outpouring, will not permanently lose its challenge. His optimism, out of tune with our dismal sciences, will be felt again as the poet's due share of the Creator's joy: " And God saw everything that he had made, and behold it was very good." And a generation amorous for many-coloured humanisms, will not long neglect that virile genius which delved to depths of the personal consciousness and of human secrecy, which could work a prophet's revelation for the infinite consequence, the mystery of each blind human vortex, for the potential worth of each grotesque fragment of humanity, its utter difference from its fellows. We may with Mr. Santayana judge Browning the pioneer vandal of verse-disintegration, or with M. Jusserand, " *sans comparison l'âme la plus haute et la plus forte que compte la poésie anglaise depuis Shakespeare.*" But spite of the clubs there will always be something new to be said about Browning.

Edward Fitzgerald used to complain that in the company of one special friend his spirit was rebuked to a somewhat overmastered meekness. I fancy he would have felt the same about Browning. We are sure to value most choicely an intimacy with a high genius but are quite as glad to see again those old comrades worthy of our steady affection whom we can hail unabashed by too profound a reverence. In bookland, too, we are sometimes more at ease with lesser folks. A proved mind there always is here and there, pure and large of a sort, but too complaisant to contemporary taste to be passed on to the next age save as the author of a single book or at most of two. Shy folks there are who keep their privacy too far apart from the onward movement of the time to go forward in the centre of the current. And if we find these too at the century's touch better and bigger than we had guessed, the pleasure of our meeting has added the flavour of a gratified vanity that we had the gift to know them. So has it been with the translator of Omar, himself.

It was the centennial which some time ago unburied from beneath the weight of the *Rubaiyat's* terrible popularity that savant, hermit, musician, gypsy, artist, fisherman, friend, Edward Fitzgerald. No doubt he would shrink from our prying even as in his lifetime he constantly laughed at his " fine parts " and " great works," concealed his little adventures in print with proud shyness, and withheld from a peering future the intimate relics of his personality. More retiring than Kipling's muskrat Chuchundra, who could never make up his mind to run into the middle of the room, he guarded with careful pains the freedom of his " invisibility," fled even from the friends for whom he hankered if he must risk for them " the sight of a new face in polite circles." Yet it is easy to understand the hearty remembrance in which he was held by the famous friends who could beguile him from his obscurity, Spedding, Laurence, Frederick and Alfred Tennyson, Thackeray. And perhaps we can better appreciate his quality today when the fine old connoisseur has so nearly given place to the less appealing person, the scholar. For Fitzgerald seems to have relished more ripely than others all things clean and rare under the sun and the light of his own whimsical fancy, to have pictured them with a sight poetic and humorous at once, a delightful trick of odd analogy. Which was dearest, we wonder, Persian poetry or the " Old Sea," the empty sands, the turnips in their rows, the captain of his herring-lugger, the sweet field winds, the exhibits of the National Gallery for which he would now and then dodge up to London, " the merry old writers of more manly times " or the achievements of his immortal friends with which as he grew in years his anxious ambition was never satisfied. We should like to tell him that he might have spared his worry.

III

For the birthdays have already outmoded the cheap slur at Victorianism. We must substitute something else for the easy jest which served so long as handy proof of modernness and emancipation. It had sufficient sparkle when it was new. George Moore got in an early word about " Literature at Nurse " in his remonstrances against the edifying consistency of Mudie's Library. Max Beerbohm had his youthful fling at " the era of *sancta simplicitas*," in the first number of the flaunting *Yellow Book* which appears to us today so innocuous. Edmund Gosse, who lived through a large span of the elder century, spoke of its " agony " with an assumption that the funeral would be on the very next day. Mr. Chesterton, always assumed to mean something bright, talked throughout a popular book of the " Victorian compromise " without quite explaining his meaning, though it was understood by us all to be certainly a paradox. Mr. Chesterton was of course presupposing our familiarity with John Morley's noble *Essay on Compromise,* an early plea for " the moral obligation of being intelligent " or rather for the intelligent obligation of being moral; — though Morley was assailing less fundamentally his own generation than the constant penchant of human duplicity to keep in with both God and Mammon, forgetful of the purest human motive: " to increase the sum of conscientiousness in the world." W. E. Henley, who dared name anything obnoxious, called the Victorian disease " Impuritanism," compound, we suppose, of prudery and prurience.

The Victorians had, we must admit, their provincialisms. They were shocked by Charlotte Brontë; they never mentioned Fielding without apology; they always spelled damn d——. These are grave admissions. What is more, they were not in the habit of making fiction-fable or table-conversation out of sex problems. These vagaries we must allow. But we need go no further, perhaps, in humiliation. The idea has long been stirring that perhaps the Victorian really preferred to write of other things from other really genuine interests. And barring such provisos, we may respect the good folks of our late centennials in the words of a critic who shared and outlived their time, — Mrs. Meynell. In the years of their neglect she had prophecied their return: " Until we can read them as ancient history we cannot read them at all." And not long before her death she wrote her stout confession of faith for the literary giants of the mid-century: " There never was so much separate and single literature written in our language as then. They were authors steady, unboastful, related to all time, classic, romantic, new." * And time, which removes all superlatives, is nevertheless explaining her *credo*.

* Quoted from the *Dublin Review*.

All acknowledgments to the Victorian centennials! They have made miracles more real than the magic lore of the fairy tales. For what less than a miracle ever happens when " fresh flowers spring up from hoarded seed " and a new season begins for life once harvested and stored, come out to leaf again under the sun? The associations of a literary centennial are not to be put aside when it is past — to lie unhandled for a hundred years. In the fairy tale, when the day is over, the suddenly awakened castle turns again to stone, the little village sinks again with its ephemeral bustle once more to the depths of the ground. But the beauty of old books remains with us, like bodies of martyrs found instinct with life and sweetness after burial. The centenary has been not a memorial but a renaissance.

CROTCHETS

I

THE WOOD OF REAL BEASTS

I

" Viens donc voir dans les bois de véritables bêtes! "

HERE was a kindly bidding which has been most unkindly disregarded. It is still, so many years after Rostand's death, a bold deed to choose a text from *Chantecler*. " Noah's ark become menagerie," we have been told to call it, " a medley of whimsies and puns." Very likely the discriminating are partly right in their tiresome way. But some of us remember to have sighted around the corner of the menagerie a glimpse of an immemorial wood, to have caught beneath the " verbal caprice and satirical trifling " a word of authentic incantation, the lucky formula for the recovery of an ancient kinship — the right beastly invitation:

" Viens donc voir dans les bois de véritables bêtes! "

O wood of real beasts! Who could choose instead the Garden of the Hesperides or the Islands of the Young?

Children know surely of the wood. I myself was an unpleasantly skeptical child. I scouted the notion of gold at the rainbow's foot. I suspected from the first that Jack-in-the-pulpit never preached. But at night, when my uncle told me stories of bears, I preferred to sit close on his knee, facing in the direction of our urban grove that no bear might take me unawares from behind. It was a delicious danger. For the beasts of the wood are real.

They are knowing, too. Wisdom, as the fables plainly showed, was more signally developed in the animal world. Moral instruction was less unwelcome from the tortoise, so slow yet so persistent, from the ant, so industrious yet so interesting, than it would have sounded in any human persuasion.

Wise or not, the society of Brer Rabbit was a better adventure than the companionship, august but somehow less homelike, of a golden-haired princess or of a prince disguised as a dragon. Even so inconsiderable a beast as Puss was worth more in boots than any other creature so accoutred. What would Red Riding-hood count without her wolf? What should we care for Goldilocks without her dreadful animal attendance? And the one fairy tragedy which haunted me inconsolably in the wonder days — which haunts me still — is that sad affair of the mermaid who achieved her soul at the expense of her tail. For the ways of men with souls, as they say, stray far from the free wild ways. And a word of disenchantment, too, we have from Rostand:

" *Chut! Baissez le rideau vite! Voilà les hommes!* "

If in our grown-up years we can still find the password to the real wood, it is good for us to be there.

In the pride of our spiritual prestige we may conceive
that by favour of evolution we have climbed " upward, leaving out the beast." In our more aspiring
reckonings of human destiny we have been wont, till
of late we lost the right, to recoil at a nature " red in
tooth and claw." But with the smell of the clean
woods beyond the world, with the first shock of the
forest stillness, at the first crackle of underbrush or
glimpse of a low brown body leaping across the path,
a primal instinct still awakens for our health. For
the time it is ambition enough to " foot at peace with
mouse and worm."

That is no small ambition. For whoso would penetrate the outer rim of the forest world is soon stripped
of his urban complacency. At home in our back gardens, perhaps, we may safely sun ourselves in our
lordship above other creatures. We are gardeners,
and apparently can, by taking thought, add a few
inches to the tomato vine. Or if we would assert more
aggressively our powers, we can tell the dog to come
and he will sometimes come. But if we would win
our way to the confidence of the quick-panting forest folk, we must bear ourselves right humbly. Our
diminishing importance is more salutary for the re-
storing of our souls than weeks in the greenest of
village pastures. However masterful we may be in
the pride of Adam's inheritance, we have not au-
thority enough to persuade the fat woodchuck to
stop for a moment in his heavy scramble. We are inconsiderable for all our upright posture.

A chipmunk was the first to put me properly in my

place — no debased semi-chipmunk of the dusty turnpike but a frisker of the beechen forest by a mountain lake. Here the spectacle of aërial change, the miracles of lake and mountain, could be taken happily for granted; there were greater concerns for attention. The event of the day began with the scudding scamper which announced that the neighbour of the broken cedar was undertaking his daily condescension and maybe would consent to eat out of my hand. For at touch of the little cold feet cautiously trustful, at the climbing pull of the light, curved body, I felt admitted to nature's gentility, seized of the soggy soil of the ferny wood. So I set great store by the chipmunk's favour, and marveled in simplicity at the elfish transformation as the sharp face rounded to the cobra's head while the cheek filled with its overload. If he brushed my foot, it was a notable occurrence; if he leaped to my shoulder, it was an experience to register; if he bit an obstructing finger as he pushed a strong nose into the curve of the hand, compliment could go no further. Mowgli may have felt lifted up in heart when he was made free of the jungle, Chantecler when he flew from the company of hens who use ladders to the wood of the pheasant and the nightingale. A friendly nip from the tooth of a forest chipmunk has been enough for me.

For with the consciousness that a little wild creature has ventured to bite us in pleasant security, there is touched some spring of gentleness, the best of woodland gifts. Here is testimony to our essen-

tial harmlessness; here is kindly proof that once for
a moment we have been acquitted of human ruthlessness. There was much besides of manners to be
learned from the squirrel's discipline — to go on pad-
ding foot without unhallowed disturbance, to hold
my peace unless I had aught to say, to approach a
friend in front, never from behind with sudden
brusquerie. But most salutary was the assurance
given by his trust — that for humankind the ultimate, if not the primordial, virtue would be to pass
among created things, blameless of mischief. For
the moment I had risen serene above the contempt of
our fallen state, had gone back to the time when
Adam and Eve walked supreme in the garden of
Eden, while about them frisked the beasts " since
wild," and the lion dangled the kid in his jaws for
the fun of the thing, and the elephant " used all his
might to make them mirth." And I understood why
our most likely symbol for a far-away millennium is
the old prophecy that the lion and the lamb shall lie
down together. Yes, I suppose in that comfortable
day man and beast, too, shall meet in the cool shades
on the border between the wood and the world, look
at each other with shy, bright eyes under the green
light, and pass on in kindliness through the sun-
flecked forest coverts.

Not for nothing does our sweet saint lore record
the favour of beasts to the pure in soul. Here is the
best way to test a saint, though the signs for detec-
tion be many and sure. Sometimes he is only hard
to kill; sometimes he can recognize the devil at sight;

sometimes he can tell of heaven. But the surest proof is to find him surrounded by the wood creatures, who have long since lost their Eden trust, drawn near to the comfort of holiness alone, once more confiding and understanding. What should St. Brandan do for his best marvel without the ministration of the little birds? How should we recognize the retreat of dark St. Guthlac praying hermit-wise in his ferny thicket — how should the angels find him for his fellowship, without the obedient groups before him, the deer and the wolf awe-struck at his bidding, tame in the presence of love alone, which overcomes man and beast? And our more familiar patron of Umbrian days, he of the Umbrian hills, is less wonderful in his gift of the stigmata than in his power to draw the birds to an audience and to keep the little fishes still. Francis himself, I suppose, esteemed a less feat his passage of the flames than the conversion of Brother Wolf.

Our unsanctified will must have in it a more modest working. In the mundane business of our degenerate days the chances are the smallest that we shall hold an animal circle intent through our holiness. It is unlikely that, however virtuous we may be, if we meet the lion by the way, he will mitigate his savage mood. Lions, alas, are as scarce as bears in the woods behind our house. Still we have our capital recollections of forest triumph to chronicle.

There are some, of course, who cherish the exultation of less tangible experience. They have caught perhaps some vision seldom vouchsafed of nature's more exalted beauty, have felt themselves the chance centre of special cosmic arrangements. Browning's feast of Transfiguration was the moon rainbow of his *Christmas-Eve,* sprung to sight for him, " one out of a world of men." I, too, have seen my moon rainbow, a dim aërial arch over a surging lake. I, too, shall remember a persuasion of special privilege, as if I had chanced, being inadvertently overlooked by the powers of the air, to be present at the creation of a rarer light. But a more homefelt joy has come with the cold little touch of my mountain chipmunk. And there have been other triumphs.

There was the flitting second when the blue damsel fly, mistaking me for an abortion in the thistle world, would settle on my knee for a flick of the fine steel tracery. There was the lazy hour beneath the apple tree when the small striped snake wriggled slowly around my hat-brim so incommodiously situated over his dugout. There was the cruel morning, of which I do heartily repent, when I sat on the home of the square gray mole to watch the recurrence of his disappointed returns. There was the quivering noon by the iris field, when the muskrat who lives by the brook below my perch would rattle the stones behind the light meadow rue. There was the proud encounter with the eight little woodchucks squatted in linear exhibition in the sunshine.

" And there's a field of many, one," the sloping field along the hill's dip, where my resemblance to a stump has fooled even the yellow fox. Here under cover of the morning rustle he would steal almost to my feet and then curve aside without a start, assured that I had not seen him, so quiet had he been. And here at sunset, at the rosy moment given to those who can bear to turn their backs upon the west, I have seen him loping along through the blowing grass blossoms into the darkening acres below.

And "I know a bank where" Brer Rabbit lives. We could never grow intimate, but we have the same taste in banks — always with a thicket beside for safety — a sun-scorched tract with good store of tangle, the plumping blueberry and withholding vine, opening between the dusk and shimmer of pasture trees to the sweep of the mountain beyond. We could never really meet, my scurrying neighbour and I, being both rabbit-hearted, never standing upon the order of our going if we chanced to startle each other. But often, as I have looked back just in time to see the last wiggle of the white bunch tail, I have remembered to my sorrow that those who fear never get into society " in the woods of Westermain."

II

Nowadays it is not always easy to find the wood, and some there are who never find it.

Nimrod and his rangers will never get there. They may set forth with terrible intent, accoutred in the most ominous of huntsman panoply; they may penetrate the wild as free and far as ever the naked savage ran; they may startle the silences by the crackle of their superior frightfulness, and return, when they have borne their conquests far enough, to pose in any chance Yahoo-land as lords of the beasts once more. But in the forest, too, as surely as among the man-pack, the invader is not the guest-friend, nor can he receive the hospitable gifts of peace.

Nor is there better luck for timorous Miss Muffet when she ventures to take the field. Untaught in sylvan meekness, she shrinks on her way, thinking herself the superior morsel of the summer. She will never learn to love the small things of the air. They would never stoop to bite her, if she did but know it. For a more toothsome purpose " the fresh young fly " swings himself strongly up the tansy's side; for a sweeter store the tumbling honeybee sprawls his yellow bulk so thoroughly into the curve of the rounded clover; on better hunting the bright needle-folk from Flatland, red, brown, blue, and black, hang by a green nose beside her or rest on her knee for a fastidious second before they are off for a more natural flower. Even the menacing dragon-fly from Brobdingnag has set his mind on livelier ends, as he strikes his swift way, undecided, through the air, waking a shrilling in the trees, till he knows at last where he would be and is off with a sudden lunge. And there is no snare at all in the spotted flame of the pulsing butterfly wings wavering slowly over the thistle-top. She will never learn to love " the things that glide in the grass," painted things, shining things, which pursue their acrobatic way, oblivious of her monstrous invasion. She will never discover how carefully the colour schemes are ordered in the low-growing underworld. She will not wait to study the gay coats of the nimble field spiders, gray to shoot along the hoary crisp of the gray moss, black to scramble across the dark stone ledges, green to swing themselves over the fine curves of the light grass beneath the trees. And if once she catches sight of the giant super-spider of the inner wood, green mossy cushion in a shady hollow, which suddenly takes to itself legs for a portentous crawl among the red pine needles and the steeples of Indian pipe, she will look a long look for once, but she will never look again in the real woods.

Yes, there is no entrance to nature's fellowship for Nimrod or for Miss Muffet. The shudder and the shot are equal signs that paradise is lost. From midsummer Eden the predatory and the squeamish are alike taboo. For the woodland grace has offered them gentleness in the shifting sunshine and they have not perceived the light; it has drawn near in their little brothers of the field and wood and they have not known the kinship.

Still less chance is there for eager Actaeon, the over-prying, who would dare, if he might, to gaze upon the naked loveliness of nature. He would venture with unhallowed presumption to press too rudely for the privilege forbidden, would invade the inner shrine of earth's mysteries for a share of earth's spiritual secrets. One is sorry for the sensitive Actaeon, sinning not in negligence but in desire. The simpler offenders besides are become less frequent. Nimrod grows yearly less baleful, more scientific;

Miss Muffet we have lived to see faring afield in khaki to study the spider kind. But still we repeat the folly of Actaeon, the over-bold. Diana may have given up hunting in the modern world, though if she bathes ever in a clear forest pool, I fancy I know just where. But whatever the old story said, Actaeon is with us yet, and in human shape forever.

Forever we are teased by the secret of earth's awful beauty. We must be always leaving our simplicities to strain sight and sense toward an unimaginable wonder almost ours for the guessing. In some lighted moment it is almost caught, swept for a second before our eyes — then lifted away on a change of the wind, baffling, always ahead. We would fain perceive for ourselves the " bottom of the monstrous world "; we would " quite make out the sun," comprehend the perpetual shadow which dwells in the heart of sunshine. We shall never manage it, but we must still be trying — peering.

To enter the real wood, as we are told of the kingdom of heaven, we must not try officiously hard. Welcome is not given on demand. Only such as do not seek may find. He who would pass must be a lover of the quiet, stilled to an interior calm. Only so can he detect the multitudinous whisperings of the far-brought silence, respond to each delicate fall of the midsummer rustle, catch the earth's hidden processes with the leisure of the trees as they build their bark. So at last can he know the waiting peace of the high open spaces. He must be a lover of the sun in its heat, on the clean, dry slopes of the uplands. He must not shrink from the baking ridges where the air quivers beyond the blue pine shadows, where rises an incense charged with the fragrance of summers past — sweet fern transformed, and the seasoned pine needle and crisp strawberry vine returned to the earth which gave it. He can enter best at summer's high moment, when the thrushes are still and only one harvest fly has yet found voice for the August chanting — in the brooding hour of the noonday hush, when the wind dies down and the birch tops slacken their free morning motion. And there comes a pause in the woodland business, and the silence hovers in the light. Then to the seekers who have abandoned the search, who have ceased to listen for articulate utterance in nature's whispers, in the hour when there is no question, the secret may be opened. They may touch the gigantic indolence of growth, may feel the energy of the unhasting sun, may neighbour, but for a moment, the eternal goings-on of nature in all her creatures. And perhaps, who knows, the real divinities may be plain at last.

Presences as dear, at least, appear sometimes even to the uninitiate who are not over-eager. For as I sat one day in my mossy hollow among the thistle stalks and the pink-tipped birch sprouts, under the early sun, content in the passiveness of the goodly morning, happy in sensations which I mistook for meditations, there sounded a wheeze and a scuffle, and I knew that the real beasts were about. The deer, who came so seldom, had passed me close. And the doe stood before me on the open ridge which rose from

my feet, under a bright, swift cloud, between the
pines and the sleek birch shimmer. She stood, taut
and shapely, high head pushed out, big ears alert
that could hear so much more than I of woodland
business, bright eyes affrighted at my very harmlessness. Then with a forward plunge of the fine,
strong neck, and a scornful switch of the light tail,
and another scared wheeze, she was off and down
though the hollow.

.   .   .   .   .   .

I was not left long in my ruefulness. A distant
ringing of voices came down the hill through the
morning air. It circled me close with a growing
clamour, and my fellow boarders defiled gaily over
the ridge where the doe had stood. They had come
to pay me a visit, and they seated themselves about
in a friendly circle. One was a bird-lover, and she
was so good as to identify for us every forest call.
Another, poetical of fancy, was sure that my nook
was a fairy ring and drew for our delight the images
of tricksy sprites under the mushroom growth. Another, of classical predilections, felt that she could
catch sometimes in the dusk beyond the gleam of a
long nymph limb or hear the stir of Pan's foot in the
thicket. My chance was gone. I must take up the
white man's burden again. I would go up with them
and finish my knitting on the piazza.

" Chut! Baissez le rideau vite! Voilà les hommes! "

II

THE YOUTHFUL SPINSTER

I

THE other day, as I was poking in a neglected drawer stored with the "souvenirs" which children lay up for solace of the arid wastes ahead — frayed paper napkins once sacred to the memory of coloured ice, laced valentines of a richness not to be found nowadays, — I turned up from a dark corner the yellowed manuscript of a story which I must have written long ago. A quite forgotten thing once cherished, freshly discovered, has always a haunting attraction. But as I read, I felt that I had come upon a deposit interesting for its own sake. It was a romance — for I was probably seven at the time of its composition — and concerned the notable adventures of two fair heroines, Gwendolen and Genevieve. The tale must once have been regarded as a masterpiece, for it was carefully tied up with beautiful red cord, and illustrated with unique drawings of Gwendolen and Genevieve in Assyrian perspective, splendidly provided with bustles and dolmans of the latest mode. And after these years of eclipse the document still preserves one excellence which even in the initial pride of authorship I fancy I did not suspect, — an unashamed candour, a singular absence of guile. The last sentence alone is sufficiently telling. It ended: "And so they were both married, and had good rich husbands."

Here is conciseness perhaps crudely abrupt, but the phrases ring true with a sincerity hard to get at a later age. It is the plain expression of childhood's ideal and definite intention. For children, we notice, strangely compounded of matter-of-fact and fancy, take marriage as much for granted as bread and butter. Scant tolerance would be theirs for the fairy tale if it failed of its right conclusion, if the prince by a reversal of nature's laws should neglect to wed Cinderella. And in the cycle of their recurring games the children are consistently devoted to Hymen. They circle the ring-around-the-rosy in a rhythmic rehearsal of coquetry and wooing, and count daisy petals to a chant of love's experience. They are noisiest, we admit, in their ubiquitous dramatization of "Teacher," — teacher, poor thing, an old maid ogress promiscuously shaking little children. But there is a special unction and solemn relish in their style whenever they play at being married.

It is plain too that they pity the poor creature who can no longer join the wedding game with conviction, for they treat her with an elaborate delicacy suitable to her disappointments. The coarse term, old maid, would surely stick in the throat even of the untutored. They never use it in our presence, though I have heard "aunt maid" as a gentle euphemism. If they must mention before us our unhappy state, they hurry on with the same nonchalance which conveys to a cross-eyed or bewigged visitor the assurance that the anomaly really does not show. The " aunt maid " must want a husband, they are persuaded, but they do their best to spare her feelings by a careful affectation that they have not found her out.

The grown-up world used to hold jocundly the same opinion. In the old frank days of merry England Chaucer's hen spoke up confidently for all women, saying:

> " Whatso any woman sayth,
> We all desiren, if it might bee,
> To han housbondes hardy, wise, and free."

And being once reminded of Chaucer, we find it hard to ignore the Wife of Bath and her tale of a knight who quested for a year and a day that he might report to Queen Guinevere what thing it is that women most desire. He had a lively search, but his answer proved at the time to be the right one: " My liege lady," said he, " generally women desire to have mastery over husbands and lovers ":

> " In al the court ne was ther wyf, ne mayde, ne
> Wydwe, that contraried that he sayde."

That was a long time ago. Today the audacious youth would not get off so easily before any gathering in the " regne of femynye." Still as in Jane Austen's period " it is a truth universally acknowledged that a single man in possession of a good fortune must be in need of a wife." But the single woman is no longer conversely in need of the " good rich husband." The world has grown cheerfully to accept without smile or hint at a ceremony called "*nolo episcopari*" protestations of maidenly content. We may flaunt without ridicule our praises of independence void of " followers " or encumbrances, the joys of unhampered freedom. It is obviously convenient to walk in the middle of the path, to sit directly under the lamp, to reflect on the superior system and firmness with which we could bring up the children of others. And spite of Dante, it is not so bad to " go up and down another's stairs " with no responsibility for rolls of dust accumulating in the corners. We are believed.

II

Still the children are in one way right in their commiseration. Through some convention of society it is no longer the thing for us to appear genuinely old, though the married may age as fast as they please. Oh, to have lived with Charlotte Brontë, when one woman could write to another, "At twenty-three you can hardly call yourself young! " In that good time by twenty-five we should have sat down restfully for the remainder of our days, emancipated and relieved.

Not so today! On the head of the married gray hairs are venerable, badge of acceptable service, but we have to devise new ways to turn our hair inside outside to bring the white on the under side. The married may amble leisurely along the way or stroll quietly in pleasant by-paths. We have to step off brisk and pert to show how much strength and oil is still left in our poor old bones. The married may survey with complacence a moderate increment of plumpness, pursue calory-counting merely as a domestic grace. We must follow with the devotion of the one-time alchemist that modern unattainable, the slimming elixir of life. It is permitted to the married to seek the fellowship of wise folks older than themselves, to acquire the mellowness of their more assured repose. We are perforce ambitious for the society of " the old young girls," must seek for special familiar some pretty young thing without a gray hair in her head.

Some time ago a newly married friend sent me her book-plate, very unpretentious for a book-plate, — just a little cut of her library. I suppose there were shelves and books in the picture. I remember only two central features, a pug-nosed dog and a cordial fire-place. Here no doubt on snug winter evenings there are two more present with the tutelary dog, carelessly whiling the hours in receptive fire-side chairs. With me it is different. I too should like to sit by the register in my boarding-house and doze at my ease. But no, I am young, and I must go out and play bridge or something more youthfully inconsequent. Or if the thermometer is way below zero, I stagger half a mile through the drifts in the company of my active friends, the lads of eighteen, to witness a basket-ball game. I am so fond of athletics, like all young people.

And yet what should be in this youth, that we cling to it so tightly? It was a busy time disquieted by heavy problems. So many abstruse speculations, including axioms and platitudes and unimaginable mysteries, had to be settled out of hand, as if the weight of the future depended upon our immediate decision. What are the comparative merits of Shakespeare and Browning? Where is the border between spirit and matter? What is the relation of tragedy to comedy? Is the human will free? I remember that once in college days, as I was lounging with a book, a class-mate suddenly leaned over my shoulder and began, " Say, I never happened to ask you, but do you consider life worth living? " She felt that she must know before night. I had a glib answer in a minute, and we dealt ably with the matter. I should not feel equal to it now.

Then there was the worse responsibility of youth's privilege, the persuasion that we must make the most of our choice susceptibilities before the torpor of middle age should dull our keenness. We had to be so exquisite and so sensitive, to thrill our utmost with all fine subtleties and nice emotions. Max Beerbohm has mentioned the blight set upon the Oxford of his youth by the necessity of living up to the Pater cult of aesthetic intensity. In my college time, too, Pater was the rage among the inner intelligentsia and imposed an earnest stress upon youthful ardours. How to be kindled from that " hard, gem-like flame "? How to get as many pulsations as possible into a given instant? " Not to discriminate every moment some passionate attitude in those about us, and in the very brilliancy of their gifts some tragic dividing of forces on their ways, is, in this short day of frost and sun, to sleep before evening." Oh, the insidious and perpetual danger of the afternoon nap, that ultimate treachery to youth and opportunity!

The poets gave more lasting torment. All literature to my greedy quest echoed and reëchoed with the immemorial urge to gather the immediate rose before life should enter, as it must almost at once, the deserts of vast eternity in which roses have no future blooming. Behind me, I knew, always drawing closer, "Time's winged chariot" was hurrying. I guess today that Horace and Catullus and all the rest of them were at least in the thirties and sustained by the Roman equivalent of easy-chair, cigarette, and after-dinner coffee, while they piped of youth and love and rose in the comfortable assurance that they were already over. But how could I suspect that at eighteen?

> " Age, I do abhor thee!
> Youth, I do adore thee!
> Age, I do defy thee! "

I must hasten on, resisting every lure of the afternoon nap, to take the present time in acquisitive solemnity and conscientious anguish.

The moderns were even more depressing, for they spoke my own language of egotism and self-consciousness:

> " Verse a breeze mid blossoms straying,
>   Where hope clung feeding like a bee,
>   Both were mine! Life went a-Maying
>   With Nature, hope, and poesie,
>   When I was young! "

So chanted Coleridge to my troubled ear:

> " When I was young?
>   Ah, woful when!
>   Ah for the change 'twixt Now and Then! "

I could have imagined it very well even if the " Ode
to Dejection " had not told me. But I knew that
by heart too, and waited anxious to take my turn at
middle-aged stolidity, at the " stifled, drowsy, un-
impassioned grief " appointed for the elder soul
which should have outlived its sensibility, at the
" wan, and heartless mood " in which poetic imagination should be ultimately quenched. Never did I behold in the evening west a certain " peculiar tint of
yellow green "; never did I watch the stars behind
the flakes of cloud in a moving sky — without the
haunting reminder:

> " I see them all so excellently fair,
>   I see, not feel, how beautiful they are! "

Had it come? Was I already like that? Or was
there still reprieve, still some narrow margin of appreciation before the apathy should set in and I
should forever see beauty without feeling it? I set

the limit in the early twenties. For there was Youth's Enchiridion, Wordsworth's Ode with its alleged " Intimations of Immortality," with its far more explicit intimations of mortality's imprisonment within the body of this flesh. There was the same testimony, even more ominous from a poet of stable equilibrium:

" The thing which I have seen I now can see no
more! "

Coleridge ate opium and was otherwise flighty; but Wordsworth would no more than nature betray the mind that loved:

" The sunshine is a glorious birth,
But yet I know, where'er I go
That there hath passed away a glory from the
earth! "

I gathered my clouds of glory tight about me, looking back from time to time, lest some nebulous wisps should be already separating from the diaphanous investiture. It was the garb of my brief priesthood in the church of nature. Right ahead was the light of common day over a world of noisy years; for Wordsworth had charted with some definiteness the progress of the soul's decline. It was no adequate comfort to hear that I might develop a human heart under the sober colouring of later experience. What had I to do with the primal sympathies and the philosophic mind? I wanted my clouds of glory. I

would guard forever my bright shoots of everlast-
ingness.

A young friend once confided to me her impatience
that she could not go immediately to Europe while
she still had left some bit of sensibility, some re-
maining shred of aesthetic appreciation. And we
were all as anxious, as eager to miss no slight vibra-
tion as was the man who could never learn how to
shiver.

III

Well, we have had our experience, and it has
brought a freedom at which we should once have
shuddered. We have had our days in Europe and
detected some lingering capacities for enjoyment.
But when the summer freshet of adventuring youth
has flooded our gallery too insistently, we have
slipped away quite contentedly to bargain for coral
pins. We have known the Alpine miracle for our own,
but when the clouds have shrouded the pinnacles too
heavily, we have spread our playthings on the floor
with surprising resignation, and solaced ourselves
very happily with our carven spoons and wooden
bears. At home again in our library, we have ventured every now and then very openly upon a silly
novel, without the smallest scruple lest we shorten
thereby " the stature of our souls." Or in musical off-
hours we let Beethoven rest, assured that he will
manage very well without us, and turn to something
easy on the radio. We venture sometimes to be interested in dinner, are frankly pleased with asparagus.

A fat and slippered middle age can really be a most comfortable thing.

Could we not, then, by a bold originality, dare to accept the relief of avowed aunt-maidenhood, find solace in the enfranchisement which comes with gray hairs and plumpness and the good custom of mature fellowship? Why suffer the patronage of pity when we are so consciously able to pity in our turn the anxious follies of the more radiant age? As for me, the way appears more clear at last. I have resolved to free myself from the thraldom of youth. I have nearly decided to be just as old as I am. If I could be eighteen again, I could not accept the conditions more profoundly or settle eternal questions in time to catch an earlier train —

Youth, I do defy thee!

III

HOW DIGGING BEGAN

THE sound conservative who prefers to think of a world finished once for all, warranted not to move or to develop, might find satisfaction in exhuming a forgotten Eden tale of the early sixteenth century, innocently known, or rather unknown, as Barclay's " Fifth Eclogue." Here is to be recovered an account of creation at least as static as in the narrative of Holy Writ, with additional reassurance concerning the final and divine ordinance of existing classes. There is in the rugged lines no notion at all of irony, but they present with naïve and unconscious daring a theory of social origins as diverting as the mind of Anatole France could contrive for the race of the penguins. Here was comfortable creed for the easier centuries before the voice of Demos was heard in the land. It was a tale apt for pleasant hours in days long gone ere the reformer was " born to vex us." Common man was put right in his place and set down therein rather hard.

Shorn of rough spelling and uncouth word, the story still sounds with the simplicity of days " when Adam delved and Eve span." There is no moral issue, no subtle serpent, no fall from obedience. At least one version of the universe, we are happy to find, has made no attempt to justify the ways of God to man. The earning of bread by hard means, labour in sweat of the brow, is but the result of a mistake. Eve of course was to blame, but she certainly meant well.

The beginning reads like the story as we know it:

" First when the world was formed in creation,
  And Adam and Eve were set in their station,
  Our Lord conjoined them both as man and wife,
  To live in accord the season of their life."

By this genial version our Father Adam had in Eden a very happy family, for God —

    " Commanded mankind to multiply,
      By generation to get them progeny."

And the generation of a healthy race was no curse, no hard doom for the multiplication of sorrow. It was the joyous business of Eden. Eve did not shrink from her responsibilities. She liked her children well. Nor is there more than a hint of a tragic apple. We might all be united today as far as the apple was concerned. Moreover labour was pleasant in Eden till the fatal visit of the Lord of Creation, which turned quite accidentally into a visitation:

" The while that Adam was pitching of the fold,
  Eve was at home and sat on the threshold,
  With all her babies and children her about,
  Either in her lap within or else without.
  Now had she pleasure them hugging and kissing,
  And then was she busy them cleaning and combing."

All was joy till the coming of the Creator and the division of the children of men:

> " At last our Lord upon the fifteenth year
>   To Eve our mother did on a time appear."

Misfortune struck, as it always does, on a pleasant day. Eve had just been especially happy with her babies — busy, by a custom which we can bear to find obsolete, " with butter to anoint their necks." But alas!

> " In the meantime, while she was occupied,
>   Our Lord drawing near she suddenly espied."

Eve was very naturally in a flutter. And here, too, as in Genesis, she was ashamed, but only at the size of her family. Hence her scramble and ill-advised concealment. For it must be confessed that there was in the mother of all women a certain disingenuousness about her children:

> " And all ashamed, as fast as ever she might,
>   She hasted and hid some of them out of sight,
>   Some under hay, some under straw and chaff,
>   Some in the chimney, some in a tub of draff.
>   But such as were fair and of their stature right,
>   As wise and subtle reserved she in sight."

We cannot wonder at her nervousness. " The Father and Lord omnipotent " appeared to be a variable and arbitrary God, a combination of Cheeryble brothers and Browning's Caliban. One could not be sure of

suiting Him. But He came this day in a mood wholly
benevolent — just to see the children and, as is the
wont of visitors, to give them something. And He
said:

> " Woman, let me thy children see.
>   I come to promote each in his degree."

Eve was not unnaturally " amazed," but hurried
forward her most presentable.

> " God on them smiled and them comforted so,
>   As we with birds and dogs used to do."

He is a God who likes pretty children; and the gifts
are forthcoming straightway, no less than " the
honours belonging to mankind ":

> " At last to the most old of all
> He said, " Have thou the scepter of Rome imperial.
> Thou art the eldest. Thou shalt have most honour.
> Justice requireth that thou be emperor."
> Then to the second He said, " It is seeming
> That thou be exalted to the honour of a king."
> And unto the third He gave such dignity
> To guide an army and noble duke to be."

And so forth to the others as they were in degree.
According to the original divine plan, apparently,
everybody was to lord it in some fashion over everybody else.

Eve, delighted at the unlimited shower of benefac-
tions, grieved, as well she might, for the unlucky

children tucked away — a whole troupe of little Esaus. Was there to be no blessing for them? Without stopping to consider their appearance she made haste to drag them from their hiding-places. If they had not been prepossessing to begin with, they were not improved by their late experience:

" Their hair was rugged and powdered all with chaff,
  Some full of straws, some others full of draff,
  Some with cobwebs and dust were so arrayed
  That one beholding them might be afraid."

And the temper of the Lord was changed as He beheld them:

" Our Lord smiled not on them to show His pleasure,
  But said to them with troubled countenance,
  ' Ye smell all smoky, of stubble and of chaff,
  Ye smell of the ground, of weeds, and of draff.' "

There are no gifts for such dirty children as these. The Lord has a daintier sense for the fitness of things, though He is as anxious as Milton's God about His reputation for omnipotence:

" I shall not, although I well can,
  Of a foul villein make a gentleman."

And so the curse descended — the curse at last, though only upon a limited number of the children of men:

" Ye shall be ploughmen and tillers of the ground;
  To pain and labour shall ye always be bound.

Some shall keep oxen, and some shall hogs keep,
To dig and to delve, to hedge and to dyke,
Take this for your lot and other labour like.
To drudge and to drivel in works vile and rude,
This wise shall ye live in endless servitude.
To stoop and to sweat and subject to become,
And never to be rid of bondage and thraldom."

There was to be no nonsense, no compounding with strikes:

"Then bade He them be tough,
And never to grudge at labour or at pain,
For if they did so, it should be thing in vain."

Alas for the digger and delver!

"Thus said the Lord and Father omnipotent,
And then He ascended up into the firmament!"

IV

THE GHOST OF THE GRIND

I

I WANT Matilda to like her work, but I don't on any account want her to be a grind! " said an " alumna mother," as she confided her freshman daughter to the general mercies of our college and to my special fostering. She had saved for the last this her word of most anxious solicitude. I had been bidden to remove Matilda to a better dormitory if she should feel herself not quite congenially placed. If she should find German too taxing, I was to arrange for the substitution of something easier — literature, for example. If I should judge her to be getting worn as the term advanced, I must see that she went home earlier for the Christmas holidays. But as my good old friend, wistful in noble planning for her daughter's perfect womanhood, went questing back among the traditions of years ago to be sure that no precaution had been omitted, a large-looking fear took shape. Whatever happened, Matilda should never be a " grind."

I reflected, as I listened, with some ruefulness and more amusement, that the child is mother of the woman, in prejudice at least. And here was surviving a venerable prejudice from the clutch of which no one of us could claim exemption. If I should send out among my academic contemporaries a questionnaire to ascertain the number among them of unqualified " grinds " such as our undergraduate fancy conceived, I should discover that every one would " rather see than be one." And as for myself I would as soon hear that in scholarship I am a " grind " as that in morals I mean well.

For, however our definitions of the creature used to differ in detail, we all agreed that she was a most unpleasant person. In appearance she was untouched by the graces. We used to call her, with a fine scorn of which we were very proud, " an earnest student." You could tell her by her unconscious gait, which " moved altogether if it moved at all," by her disregard for the straggling lock, by her dull superiority to the niceties of trimness, to the romance of fabric colour. " Her collar " was traditionally " unhooked, her shoe untied, and her whole aspect denoting a careless desolation."

In mental calibre too she was of the type which never would be missed — intellectual repository of perfectly classified and perfectly useless information, of the sort which it is never quite good form for a girl of spirit to retain exactly. She was not only " up in dates." She could identify every geological specimen from a glyptodont to the hipparionex proximus. She knew the irregular verbs of all the languages and never had to lower her voice when she approached a French subjunctive. She knew who wrote " Gorboduc " and " Handlyng Synne " and the " Testament of Cresseid." She could recite the names of all the kings of Israel. She wore her days out, nosing in the library like the toad within the stone, careless of the sun, and could be lured from her researches neither by senior elections nor by a May morning. She gave more offense to the innocent than Aristides by her unmitigated excellence.

Most of us have, I fear, an only too safe assurance that the " grind " among college girls is an extinct monster superseded by the adaptations of evolution. Any apparent recurrence of the type we take for the phantom of a preserved specimen escaped for a bit from her alcohol to act as a warning among real people. But we can't be sure. At least the story of live " grinds " is still used to frighten children. For my talk with Matilda's mother was not my first on the subject.

Such a pretty girl came to call upon me one day in my office. I had been warning her of pitfalls ahead in the primrose path. She blew in like a fresh spring wind, beamed engagingly upon me, and explained: " You see, I study just as hard as I can without being a grind. And I don't want to be a grind! " The situation was familiar enough, but her attitude toward it was significant. She had come not to seek my help, nor to deprecate my wrath — just to make me feel easy, to show that there was no fault of mine, or indeed of hers, and that we must both just be cheerfully resigned to her delightful limitations. And as I looked at her daintiness and pictured in contrast the dingy wraith which she feared to resemble, I did not argue.

Still I wished that she would risk it and study just a little harder. The chance seemed remote indeed that she would develop any undue rigours of scholarly austerity. And meanwhile one could not hope to tell her of certain lights shining in darkness which her vision could not comprehend, of a mental zest which could so easily reënforce the pleasure of her days — even of an added prettiness which might well grow in her pretty eyes with growing intellectual grace behind them. Or if the unlikely danger were not negligible — that she might from overstudy become a specially developed monster, might turn through scholarly application into a temporary dragon, the prince of all good fairy-tales would be at hand, there was no manner of doubt, to disenchant her back to beauty, if there is any precedent at all in fairy-tales. What need had there been to scare her?

And there came a twinge of compunction for my own share in floating the fiction of the grind-peril. The danger signals had been set by ourselves, the college girls of yesteryear. Our fashionable aversion to obvious studiousness, so lightly conceived and more than half assumed to fit the mild levities of the last generation, has adapted itself only too neatly to the proclivities of the present generation quite honestly disposed toward life's varieties at the boldest sacrifice of life's concentrations. We knew not what we did and, indeed, were still to do.

II

For it is a quaint paradox, if we come to think of it, that the ascription of frightfulness to the passionate student among their number comes most often from the college-bred women. Grinds of a sort are still within the ranks in the middle of life's journey, real scholars of increasing efficiency, who do not look at all like our conventional definition of the type and would give quite another account of their unpretentious activities. If their studentship be applied research in the fields of practical investigation, they have their due honour from the men for value proved. But among their old friends of academic fellowship they must be on the defensive. They must hide their attainments under a specious exterior of charm and gracious manner. In olden times the dread of feminine erudition emanated most frequently from some masculine apprehension lest the nicety of the delicate female should take blight from vulgar intellectual contact, or — worse — lest the housekeeper's knack for the perfect berry-pie should lapse before the new nonsense. Today it is the college woman of the world, zealous to secure the just poise of well-rounded character in her Matilda, who holds to the dictum or at least the affectation of Bacon — that " to spend too much time in studies is sloth."

We do not use the word grind for one another now that we are grown-up. We have invented a more opprobrious term. A scholar of mature years, certainly if she have the additional stigma of association with some college faculty, is called " an academic person." You could never fancy how you look — you who are women of the world — the patronage that twists your mouths and tilts your noses when you say that So-and-so used to be very clever but that she has grown frightfully academic. Apparently you divide womankind according to Mr. Chesterton's classification of humanity into " poets, people, and professors," throwing in with professors, as a semi-fossilized formation, all devotees of bookish labour. Even the college girl will often say very kindly of her scholarly teacher: " Why, she is human after all, isn't she? " But when you are an alumna woman of the world, you conceive that your scholarly sister settles in the course of ten years into a vegetable condition, and thereafter through about ten more imperceptibly hardens into mineral. So she dries away among her books, and her circulation gradually slows down. If you prick her, she will not bleed. If you tickle her, she will not laugh. Like the Lady of Shallott, she watches the life of real men and women reflected in a mirror. She knows only " the theory of husband and lover." So she dwells shut up in cloister, chanting chaste hymns to the cold, fruitless moon, in a decadence of monotone tranquillity.

The academic person would be the last to strike a defiant attitude. It is true that the academic person settling into a comfortable middle age near the campus of a girls' college must often shake herself out of pageantry into reality, must constantly test the wires which connect her with the outside hurly-burly where the general population grows up and grows old. Occasionally an uncommonly restive spirit will cry out with the rebellious shepherdess in the fair old pastoral, " Oh, if only a very little wolf would break in! " Yes, the academic person will not deny that her life is lacking in dramatic effect.

But she would probably be the last to understand that her calling can need defense. Her tameness she would cite as her apology for existence. She would call it excuse enough in a hasty and vocational America to uphold the tradition that study is a slow thing.

III

For our modern world, seeking always new and newer inventions for putting quick girdles round the earth, is happily occupied in its educational moments with the search for still handier methods for dif-fusing general culture. We have not hit upon the perfect device yet. We have known now for a long time that the millenium will not come when every-body goes to college. A college senior once said to me, " You can get a B.A. without knowing much, can't you? I've been thinking about it for four days." We have most of us been thinking about it for longer than that. The B.A. has not turned out to be the absolute short cut to learning. And the graduate world is pathetically full of attempted short cuts which do not quite arrive, including always second-hand expedients for instruction.

We can buy a complete manual of everything from grammar to celestial mechanics. We have long studied Gothic on the phonograph. We set great store for our French and German on the linguaphone and the speak-o-phone. We are to go on conveniently with our botany and our geology by help of the sublimated moving-picture-show. We shall receive unguessed ameliorations for our historical and literary exertions from the future resources of tele-kinesis, television, telephany, photoelectricity. And even the graduate schools of our universities can show plenty of " earnest students " who would like to acquire education as the young robin gets worms — to hold the head up and the mouth open, expecting little junks of learning to be dropped in, already cut-up and, if possible, predigested.

There may then be a more than ever necessary place, among women as elsewhere, for academic resistance to a too easy progress. There may be a more than ever necessary place, in the girl's college as in the man's, for the frightfully academic person who, though loving the touch of practical affairs, nevertheless gives scholarship her central devotion, who cherishes as a reasonable service that ardour for the things of the mind, that zest of purely intellectual curiosity, which we are wont to associate in faint-hearted moments with the lost arts of the lost centuries.

Whether we used to pose as grind or butterfly or philosopher, we all remember an intellectual experience as the essential stuff of college life. College women are intimately concerned that intellectual experience shall be preserved as the essential stuff of college future, that as opportunities for scholarship increase, the zeal for their full use shall not dwindle, that a more vitally rooted culture, indeed, shall grow more wide-spread in the gardens of young America. And culture, that "plant and flower of light," does seem to require for its health a slow and careful nurture. For the quick-growing vine, the gourd which sprang up in a night, we are told that God prepared the first worm. And since creation-twilight there have been sent grasshoppers and caterpillars innumerable for all plants good and bad.

Grubbing is tame business. A life of grubbing among books must have its narrowness. But "out of olde bokes, in good feith, cometh al this newe science that men lere"; for "a good book is the precious life-blood of a master spirit," not the dusty urn which contains his ashes.

So there may be grinds still, like Browning's grammarian, even among women, worthy of a decent funeral, because they have taken leisure through life to putter around the very little roots of the very little things of learning. And the Utopian dreamer may confess a hope for the Matilda that is to be: that the college girl of the future will discard pose of nonchalance, may be weaned by degrees from her

anxiety to make her college course " a box where
sweets compacted lie," and confess with sincerity her
temporary devotion to what the Utopians called " the
free liberty of the mind and the garnishing of the
same."

V

IN MEMORY OF LOST GREEK

I

ALL things beautiful pass away to Persephone," wrote the mourning Greek, and I fancy he believed the burden of his song. But there is a native human trust in the immortality of whatever concerns ourselves, despite the acknowledged mutability of phenomena at large. So it may never have entered the poet's mind that the liquid music of his elegy, the fair Hellenic speech itself, might pass with body's beauty and pillar's pride and the perishable loveliness of vase and amphora to the pale guardianship of " Our Lady of Shadows." But the Greek tongue is well-nigh silent now in our schools, and the richest of dead languages has lapsed from its immortality and ceased commonly to " live on the lips."

Protest grew quiet long ago. It is long since Panurge, unable to find a language familiar to his valet, tried Greek at last and was understood. It is long since Milton, declaring " heart-easing mirth " to be called in heaven Euphrosyne, registered his belief in the likely theory that Greek is the natural language of the celestial regions. It is almost as long since in the Battle of Books the Ancients made their easy conquest over the pert and upstarting Moderns. Indeed that protracted literary strife between the Ancients and the Moderns, once so comfortably balanced and apparently interminable, is fallen almost out of mind. The Ancients of to-day, should they have the effrontery to form a phalanx, would not venture into battle at all. They would simply stand in line, trusting to one of the " blind hopes " of Prometheus, the assurance that they have been proved very hard to kill. And whosoever would defend their cause must no longer speak in the manner of those who expect to be heard.

The Greek scholar has accepted without rancour his partial eclipse. I dare say he remembers in his heart the good time — still to quote Rabelais — when the ancient languages were once " to their pristine purity restored," and above all Greek, " without which one might be ashamed to count himself a scholar." But if he has not studied the humanities in vain, he has not failed to learn from them liberality of view and tolerance for new orders for efficiency. He applauds the growing vogue of modern tongues, welcome promise that the American people shall yet be raised from its linguistic illiteracy; for he knows the discipline and potential liberty to be gained from the study of language. He is the brother and promoter of historical learning; for his life, dedicated to the vitality of the past, has known the reviving vigour to be reached through that permanent contact. He comprehends the popular avidity for modern literatures; for he is the disciple of a literature which has left, even to those who know it not, an eternal legacy of strength and beauty and shapeliness. He respects the young man's alertness in the quest of new philosophies; for he guards the plenteous fountains of philosophy and knows better than we the energy and intellectual humility which may derive from that search. Man of the present as of the past, he understands the recent leap of economics to the front both in education and in publication; for he met Demos long ago in the pages of Aristophanes and knows that he is to be reckoned with. No, the true classical scholar is slow to oppose a progressive shift of college emphasis.

Perhaps he feels that the real check on Greek is less the eager modernity of the academic environment than the utilitarian pressure closing always more heavily on the secondary schools. If Greek is to have any intimate share in education, the initial steps in its study must be taken early. Though we are always told that Cato learned Greek at eighty, no one has yet explained the use he made of it. But a faraway voice speaking for Greek can hardly make itself heard in the current clamour that the public money be spent not for the refinements of the negligible few, but for firmer courses of industrial preparation which shall help the workaday pupil to earn his bread with, or better, without, the sweat of his brow. Here too the conservative respects the force by which he is dispossessed. The demand that education shall serve the common need seems to him a natural impulse of elementary justice, requiring only a provident and discreet guidance. He knows the common need better than the dictator of the present, the practical man, appreciates the more elusive values of the humanities.

To Demos, under the pressure of his hungry generations, the scholar often seems the devotee of an obsolete archaism, repository of sterile, old-world impracticalities, with whom there can be no productive issue. Discussion has grown with time more urbane on all subjects. Diomed no longer hurls his ashen spear into the side of Deiphobus. But the classical scholar, wrestling to keep his foothold in the secondary school, is likely to hear under some courteous disguise the time-honoured charge, apt for the settlement of all radical differences, " Thou are not fit to hear thyself convinced." To this unsatisfactory but irrefutable argument there is never a ready answer. The pleader for Greek must prove his fitness more humanly than by a revised dialectic.

Our schools exhibit a promising bit of inconsistency by the solicitude with which Greek culture, without its tongue, is placed before the happily progressive child.

Even the high schools put Greek art in the schoolboy's way, though he has usually more trouble than had Darius the King to " remember the Athenians." As he proceeds along the corridor in these days of ardent school decoration, he goes through a double row of masterpieces which the world has still no mind to lose. High under the cornice the Parthenon horses prance in a procession of hoofless glory. In the distance looms up an armless Venus. Above the

window headless Niké for ever tries in vain to un-
fasten her sandal. Sometimes the boy notes the
maimed deities as he passes; but frankly I suppose
he would prefer statues of a race less august but
with all their members intact. These things appear
acceptable to the educated, but for the most part, in
his opinion, they are " antiquities which nobody can
know." Yet we insist that he shall know them.

And in the grown-up world of culture the pulse of
Hellenic blood still beats high. Here the zest persists
for all things Greek except the language. The lecture
halls of notable classic scholars are thronged as
promptly as ever. Archæology, once fearfully regarded by the vulgar as a science of dry bones for
the strictly academic, makes yearly a more engaging
appeal to common man. Of books of travel in Greece
there is no end, for the ever-pressing vanguard of
the tourist hordes, finding stale its historic stamping-
ground of western Europe, long since advanced its
frontier and pushed eastward along the far Ægean
shores.

Yes, the next generation will look more familiarly,
if more profanely, than ourselves on the ruined
temples which stand for our reverence under the old
Greek sky. They will step more boldly across the
threshold of the gods, loiter at their ease in the pil-
lared porticos, and wander at will among the dese-
crated shrines. They too will love the yellowed soft-
ness of the weathered fanes standing in the curve
of many a round shore or rising in golden hill-top
light against the live blue of the southern sky. These

are beautiful things which have not yet passed away
to Persephone. They will find at Athens or at Pæs-
tum or at Girgenti a present loveliness and a fair
symbolism of departed days. But one joy they will
lack, though they praise the gods with sincerity and
venerate duly the classic shrines. They will not have
what Macaulay, supposing that he referred to a universal and enduring experience, called " our dear
classical recollections." Our children will not have
heard in old school days Zeus and Athena speaking
their own tongue in the clear temple of Hellenic
story, — a temple big enough to celebrate " heaven
and ocean and air and the imperishable race of all
the blessed gods."

II

Dear classical recollections — already the phrase
has a quaint ring! But we who have them still bear
witness that they are precious, and we think that our
witness is true. At least our testimony is not invalid
through the prejudice of our erudition; for we who
now dare wish the survival of our heritage for the
coming generations are not the classical scholars.

We are the neglectful who have passed for the
most part to other affairs, and, to speak honestly, we
have forgotten that Greek " which we so much do
vaunt but nowhere show." The grimy old books were
long ago relegated to the bottom shelf, and above
them has arisen tier on tier the library of our subse-
quent fast-slipping interests. Anacreon long since

made place for Herrick, Lucian for Anatole France, Euripides for Ibsen. Fair-armed Nausicaa has faded before the vision of Beatrice, and Cuchulain one day cut the ground from under Achilles by a single stroke. The little red dictionary in the corner is dusted no oftener than the obduracies of housekeeping demand; Æschylus, crowned not only on earth but in Hades, is growing as Greek to us as the conversation of Cicero sounded to Casca; even the pet anthology, once lightly familiar, "though much worn, is therein little read."

The Iliad still opens to the Trojan walls where heaven-born Helen passes like to one of the immortal goddesses among the aged men, or to the grim contest where the soul of Hector, defender of Trojans, is driven from the body, lamenting its bloom and its youth. But the pictures flash no longer from the words, only gleam out dimly at the sound suggestion of the noble verse. Without the little red dictionary we could hardly construe a line of Homer or chat with dear old Herodotus on the insufferable presumption of the Persians. If we would render a chorus of the "Agamemnon," we must invent the metre for ourselves, and our interpretation of Pindar must be, like Pindar himself to Cowley, a "species alone."

And yet in a most unscholarly fashion the Hellenic world has remained even for us a memory clean and potent of great old things cool and fresh, of clear simplicities and single passions, of living grace and abundant life. We stood long ago as suppliants to the blessed gods, the Lord of the Silver Bow, and Dictynna of the Mountains, and that god " wonderful by night, leader in the dance of the fire-breathing stars," and to " Earth the mother of all." We have been at the service of Bacchus, in no operatic orgy, but with Euripides in the midnight wood, while the crackle of satyr and mænad sounded nigh in the thicket, and we heard the very cry of joy when the ruddy god, the son of Semele, was born. We have rested in an authentic Arcadia, no fancy land of coral clasps and amber studs, not in court guise or ribboned masquerade or wailing a mournful threnody in the funeral train of some northern Thyrsis or Lycidas. But in a sunny Arcadia of the living we have seen the fattening of the two-year kid, have drunk pure milk from a basin round and shapely, have heard the pipes under a Sicilian sun and watched below the shifting trace of level wind on a blue Sicilian sea. We have been in Cloud-Cuckoo-Land and heard in the lilt of perfect anapests the primal twittering of birds on creation day, and believed for truth the word of the old poet that " the Graces, seeking for a support to which they might cling and not fall, found the soul of Aristophanes." And I, for one, have waited in the Vatican till I could be alone before the Far-Darter, careless that it is no longer permissible to adore Apollo Belvidere, and have addressed to him as a reasonable service the right invocation in his own language.

Our children will not quote Greek, but they can have their fill of translation. Indeed the ubiquity of cheap English versions is a satisfactorily commercial proof that the compulsion of the Greek spirit remains with us. But for all cosmopolitan tongues save the Greek it is an accepted platitude that poetry which has suffered a transmigration of language is quenched of its flavor like wine which has crossed the sea. Never are we asked to test the noble Prologue of *Faust,* unless we are strong enough to hear the morning stars and all the works of nature singing together in stout German. We do not presume to seek the ineffable vision of Dante without the support of the " fine style which does him honour." Nor can we touch the secrets of our own poets without the interpretation of their native melodies.

Chaucer, spirit of intimate cheer, we may not know without the full-voweled richness of his easy music; nor Milton, the " mighty-mouthèd inventor of harmonies," without his harmony; nor can we travel the high-rambling ways of the *Faerie Queene,* if we have not leisure for Spenser's majestic pace. How, then, is the gold become dimmed, how is the most pure gold changed, if we seek to enter too cheaply the thesaurus of classic riches, ignorant of the language which has given to our own the sacred words " poet " and " melody," and has taught us that " enthusiasm " is divine, for " a god is in it." Ours is but lip-service to that god, if we allow to dwindle into far-off spaces the true sound of Prometheus's immense invocation, or lose the veritable echo of the great " song that saved at Salamis."

There will not be another revival of Greek learning so confiding as the old, when " the ancient tongues were to their pristine purity restored." Never again will the Greek letters carry so venerable a meaning as in the early Renaissance days when, their significance guessed only by a few, they seemed occult and fraught with marvel, master-words yet to be spelled, able perchance to call to flesh again the grand and careless divinities of the elder days. Nor can Greek be to us or to our children the entrance-talisman to a brave new world of indisputable thought, unexplored country of unquestioned wisdom and reliable truth, abundant for the instruction of the nations. Centuries of scholars have explored that country, and the instruction of the nations is by no means complete. Besides, our generation hears of its unexplored countries from the complex challenge of the present, finds for its curiosity and intellectual devotion a richness of perplexity and unmeasured compass of inquiry not imaginable to the Greeks. The wholesale absorption of our master minds in the minutiæ of classic scholarship, already finely chopped through the ages, is unthinkable.

But to preserve within easy reach the mother tongue of our culture inheritance is but to safeguard an essential element of our present. We have learned in larger matters to distrust new orders which displace the past in wholesale rejection of experience; for in more ways than one the world is proved " wise, being very old." We must, to be sure, plead for our conservatisms with qualified insistence. We must not press our claims too loudly, or champion our cause

with disproportionate affection. We shall not impose
the humanities upon the unwilling and the unready.
If the growing generation asks the means of bread,
we shall not cry out upon " blind mouths " and ordain
a forcible feeding of Greek. But to urge that Greek
be restored to reasonable accessibility is not to make
a sentimental claim upon the public purse. After
all, we do not champion our classical recollections in
stiff attachment to the clustered associations of
school-days or in too rigid a loyalty to the wholesome
classic training. But with opposition our regret has
turned to full persuasion that a distinct proportion
of Greek must be guaranteed to popular education,
if we are to insure the continued efficiency of English literary scholarship or save a necessary standard
for the full enlightenment and discipline of the English literary genius.

In America at least there is needed some modest
revival of Greek learning, without which in more il-
literate times a man " might be ashamed to count
himself a scholar."

III

To call one's self a scholar requires to-day perhaps more than ever the gift of tongues; for this is
still the generation of those who seek " comparative
literature," no longer kept a mystery for the inner
circle of the initiate, but offered freely by open invitation. The critical school of judicial and oracular
pronouncement is in its grave; luckily it cannot

come out of it. Even the cult of the personal " appreciation," though we may trust its permanency, can no longer shut itself in the private chambers of its imagery to spin its web. Our more immediate zeal is to seek out the hidden sources of literary impulse, to trace through the ages the continuous action and reaction of one country upon another, anxious in a cordial spirit of cousinship to claim all our international relations. This zest for the community of literary material has been good for us. It has served to clear the overgrown channels of research, to reveal below the swirl of local detail a simplicity of advance. It has humanized us besides to transcend even a little our provincialism, to find a home-felt pleasure at each new proof of the universal kinship.

But in our ardour for a cosmopolitan scope of study we may need to guard more carefully against the large danger of the little learning. In our modern world thus frankly addicted to " genealogical criticism " we must know the languages of the genealogy. The popularization of comparative literature can easily enfeeble the grip and slacken the judgment if it is undertaken without the necessary rigours, in sluggish acceptance of pre-digested manna. Without the languages to serve our individual turn, we cannot know in miniature the experience of the pioneer scholar, or take honest satisfaction in the discovery of " a poor thing " but our own. And as we cannot with any perspicacity compare literatures seen darkly through the glass of translation, so we cannot compare their genealogies in ignorance of their be-

ginnings if anything has a beginning. We cannot return in seriousness to these beginnings and forget
that, if Latin has contributed more of its body to the
modern tongues, Greek has given a finer service of
its spirit.

And the English genius, unconfined and fancy-
free as it has liked to think itself, still needs, we may
suppose, for its perpetual correction the ripe understanding of classic restraint. Ours is the tradition of
liberty in artistic method, of vigorous exuberances
and inspired variations. And surely we have in-
dulged our native willfulness not blindly but in sound
instinct. The independence of the English nature
has been its condition of fertile and healthy production; the rich field of English letters would have
yielded a less generous growth if it had not often
outsprouted attempts at artificial clipping. But our
unfettered energies may easily become " outrageosities " if we fail to keep for reference the canons of
Hellenic classicism. And perhaps we shall indulge
our vagaries more incautiously, if the classic ideal
does not remain a steadfast witness to the rectitude
of structure behind all the lively shifts of experimen-
talism.

Ours, we are told besides, is the literature of the
personal and the particular. Ever since Chaucer
went on pilgrimage to Canterbury, it has continued
to marshal sundry folks each different in soul and
feature from every other. " Here she was wont to go,
and here, and here," sang the English shepherd; and
whoso follows the footsteps of the English muse fol-

lows a path lined with special trees and bordered by the local wayside flower. And our zest for the significant detail has served its function in the development of the world's letters. Literary evolution, at least, if it is to be " careful of the type," can never be " careless of the single life." But we shall create our individuals and our singularities with less conviction, if the touchstone of the catholic and the universal is not kept in the singleness of Greek genius.

For a century and more we have often been, like the rest of the world, voluble and inclined to confidence. Modern personality, zealous to search its inmost recesses, has not scrupled to handle the intimacies with familiarity and to give up its secret sins and revered privacies. And as we face the broader human interests, we do not grow less talkative; rather we become more eager to express the utmost of the personal thought and experience for the enrichment of the common destiny. Upon us presses the demand for the broader personality; around us throng the claims of the universal problems, asking practical and theoretical solution. Here too the responsibility which so easily besets us is, we hope, obedient to a normal right. Long ago in the old romance, Sir Percival, perversely silent before the procession of the Grail mysteries, taught the lesson that man's lasting duty in the presence of perplexing mysteries is to question their meaning. The modern world cannot ask its multifarious questions in silence. It must continue the ever-deepening murmur of query and tentative reply. We shall wait long before reticence will become for us a dominant literary note. Perhaps it may never rightly become so. But in tired hours we shall still do wisely now and then, if we return for a little to the dignified Greek world of noble withdrawal.

And perhaps as we pass farther from the repose of the classic spirit, we may but need it the more. Perhaps the poetry of the next generation, if it reaches out with more assurance in significant choice of the democratic and common subject; if, groping still toward the expression of the common need, it chooses with even more resolution the dialect of the ignorant and the vulgar, may require more than ever the reminder that sympathy of heart takes no necessary issue with serenity and dignity of tone. Certainly we shall need all the classical reminders we can get in many-blooded America, which claims as its privilege to-day in its taste for literary form — as it claimed of old for its tenets political and religious — " the dissidence of dissent."

IV

Perhaps our hope is not " blind." We must temperately bide our time till a more generous subsidy of public education shall be commonly recognized as the best patriotic investment. We must wait till the captivity of the secondary school-teacher is turned by a sufficiency of competent help to free and adequate service. We must not lay Greek as a last straw upon her devoted back, already weighted with a load which would tax miraculous virtue. We must wait in patience besides till at whatever lavishness of experimental waste we have met with a more practical intelligence the necessity of the labouring world for efficient vocational preparation. Daily are we surer that if man cannot live by bread alone, he is not likely to live without it in any way creditable to civilization.

But already in our well-intentioned doubling of courses and differentiation of systems we may be in danger of cutting the class chasm too wide. The boy even of the industrial school has the right to know that the things of culture exist, that they are excellent and are unforbidden. *Life* long ago published a capital cartoon. On the pictured bottom of the sea lay an open chest stored with gold enough to stock several Treasure Islands. Near by lingered two shrewd young fishes. " Come along," said one. " You won't find any worms there." And the gold lay, we suppose, untouched, thereafter to be unregarded. It is not the least privilege of the high school to broadcast the gospel that there are other things than worms, to assert the preciousness of the world's fine gold, and to keep open the approach to all treasures of learning for those whose happier lot or more aspiring energy allows the longer search in college years. Yet again perhaps shall Greek live on the lips.

And indeed, if we are wrong, if the stimulus of Greek is to be eliminated from the common suggestion of heart and thought, the neglect will be due in part to its past sufficiency, so intrinsically has it modified the direction of our growth. For of other gods than Brahma it might rightly be written, "When me they fly, I am the wings." If we can do without Greek, we can only think that its services have been "so splendid that they are no longer necessary."

But that we shall long forego indirect contact with this essential gift from the world's great past, the mind which has faith in the steadiness of our racial progress cannot believe. Still must the modern world give tribute of earth and water to the old. "The ancient melodies have ceased," and the "fair nine" are become wanderers on the earth. But though attempts have been made to supersede them, though a Heavenly Muse has even sat upon Mount Sinai, though we may live to see the cult of muses most unclassical, when new ways prove hard and new fountains dry, we shall return gladly and not in vain to the old invocation:

> "Hereth, that on Parnasso dwelle,
> By Elicon, the clere welle!"

VI

THE CREED OF THE CONCRETE *

I

IN these days of propaganda for lost causes one
would like to say something unobtrusive and
kind in behalf of the abstract noun. For this, one
would judge, is the generation of those who seek the
concrete. Even the good word, "to generalize," has
fallen into disrepute. It has come to be in common
parlance a term of opprobrium. It apparently means
no longer our supreme human privilege, to make
fact into thought; it means rather to choose vagueness as an outlet for slipshod apprehension. "Don't
generalize so," is our stock reproach for the evasions
of the loose and negligible talker.

The adjective of course has fairly good treatment
nowadays. Many of us remember the years when
that pleasant descriptive member was held a special
stumbling-block of callow adolescence. The taste for
a string of epithets was one of the pretty little infant
wiles to be eradicated with the greatest dispatch.
But we have learned that there is no danger here.
Our desperate struggles have never been against
over-expressiveness on the part of our children.
Even a girl prefers one superb adjective used as often

* Reprinted from the *Sewanee Review*.

as possible to the luxuriance of a string. And if there was ever a boy who carried into later life a proclivity for adjectival indulgence, he was an unusual phenomenon. One recalls Thackeray's comment on the innocence of juvenile stomachs: " Boys contract habits of tart- and toffee-eating which they do not carry into later life. On the contrary, I wish I did like 'em."

One might hazard the guess that this is specially the generation of the verb. My philosophical friend, to whom I have ventured the opinion, finds it interesting if true, and discovers in such a tendency still another indication of contemporary value for the process rather than for the end, by a rational conformity to the spirit of the time, which is more particularly than usual a " stream of time." I wish she may be right.

At any rate the verbs, since they are so very active, are appropriate for our present. We need them more and more as literature has less and less to say about still life. The " set piece " in prose has become an increasingly isolated sight. It is almost quaint to sit down and write a description unless one wants for some reason to call it a poem. Description, we are taught by the masters of those who know rhetoric today, exists in contemporary practice under the mantle of narration, for the most part implicit and absorbed in the progress of the novel. And the story perforce proceeds from move to move, whether it dashes with objective frankness from one murder to the next or zigzags the stream of consciousness in those erratic and interminable tangents so dear to the psychologists of fiction. Quite simply, our modern penchant for getting about has penetrated our literary creed and habit. We live and write to the measure of Gilbert and Sullivan:

> " Should you ask the special function
> Of our never ceasing motion,
> We reply without compunction
> That we haven't any notion."

No longer may a story commence with the honoured formula: " The youth beheld before him an extensive scene." " He stepped on the gas " is more acceptable, partly because we cheaply and naturally prefer the quick and easy, partly in reasoned respect for immediacy of effect and directness of sensuous hit. But whatever the pace, it is the verb that does the going.

The concrete noun has of course an excellent chance. Nouns must always be to go with verbs, " hand in hand," in the picturesque phrase of the juvenile. A distinct fatigue comes sometimes to the steady reader of contemporary fiction at the patter of sense impressions, the insistence almost amounting to battery upon the contacts of sight and touch. One feels the quality most sharply in a foreign language to which one is not to the manner born. Whence come those words which used not to be there when we went to school, which glow and crunch and rasp and flay and scrape with their sheer assault upon the eye and skin? And our English is not behindhand. " Literature is hard," said a small boy to me, and nowhere harder than in its merciless grip upon the flesh, in a materialism of vocabulary which is the natural conclusion of its materialistic theory and practice.

To press a counterclaim is an almost dangerous task. Concreteness has long been a literary religion. If Samuel Butler were living, he would doubtless include it in his list of the vested interests. It has been sacred for excellent reason; for it has meant the realization of the poet, it has been the worthy Mecca of many a prose pilgrimage. And still expressionism, as Mr. Ernest Boyd translates, predicts in its lust for the verb-triumphant the " de-substantivisation " of the world. The pedagogue has taken his cue from the poet and critic. The dogma — Seek the Concrete — has been chanted almost with the regularity which used to be reserved for those cold trinities, Unity — Coherence — Emphasis and Clearness — — Force — Elegance.

II

The suspicion that there can be too much even of this good thing forces itself upon the mind of the critic who listens very continuously to the conversation of the nation's youth and notes with boldness its characteristic vocabulary. The other day I inquired of two college seniors the definition of counterpoint, feigning — perhaps, to test their powers of explanation — even more ignorance than I had. They were delighted to instruct me; but their troubles over my enlightenment seemed somehow representative of well-nurtured Juventus. They began blithely to expound, using easily, as they went, a good and simple imagery to elucidate their meaning; but still I did not get an exact definition of counterpoint. They multiplied their analogies with an ingenuity that won my admiration, — delightful, original, suggestive, more informing than I admitted. But I never got my definition. The anecdote is hardly fair. None of us likes to be confronted with the order to deliver on a sudden some nice and taut distinction. Counterpoint, besides, involves the phrasing of relationship, and such vocabulary common man is content to leave to the mathematician and the specialist. Let such sages attend to " the formless, shapeless, intangible idea."

But other thought-nouns there are which ought freely to live on the lips or at least to be kept in a convenient cupboard. Abstract, as the grammar without imagination names them, they are not alien and remote, like such dread concepts as " relativity " or " infinity." Theirs was the potency, for structure, for meaning, and for resonance, in the strong old eighteenth century sentence of a Fielding or a Smollett. They are nouns of experience, qualitative, critical, humane, apt for quick interchange of our human findings. They are nouns, as it were, of relish, by which we name our " realizings " along the ways of life and companionable thought. But such as these our Juventus has mislaid.

True child of his time, he has a touch on fact. And

to him the words of fact and sense come readily. He has a store, each with its definite associated image: man, girl, car, coat, theatre, dance, ball, bat, touch-down, ice-cream, and the like. One remembers again wistfully the famous old list: " Herein may be seen noble chivalry, courtesy, friendliness, cowardice, murder, hate, virtue, and sin." But presumably none of these or of their modern equivalents would come readily to the tongue of average young folk except love and murder. The words are of course dormant, as it were, in their environment, held submerged in memory and consciousness, but not right handy where they can be automatically picked up like a handkerchief or a pair of gloves. They are not a regular part of the regular kit of regular speech.

One might venture to be frankly pedagogical for a moment, and confess the struggle of well-meaning Juventus to express with grammatical nicety any general or semi-general proposition. Take the colloquial pronoun " you " and its well-nigh universal adoption as indefinite in place of even the mildest approach to an abstraction. Once upon a time, trying to extract from a high-school freshman class some interpretation of Hawthorne's symbolic story about the water of life, " Dr. Heidigger's Experiment," I was startled by the reply: " Why, I think it means that if you should become young again, you would be just as silly as ever." If I had felt sufficiently spirited to exert myself for some modification, I should no doubt have heard, " If one should become young again, he would be just as silly as ever." If I had pleaded for a polite inclusion of the speaker within the terms of the generality, he would probably have managed at last: " If we could all in later years return to youth, we should be just as silly as ever." Certainly I alone in the room would have thought of saying, " Age shows no advance over the follies of youth." The naïveté of the above illustration would be hard perhaps to parallel in college, but to make a personal allusion out of an abstraction is a habit ubiquitous and perennial.

The finesse needed during the early meetings of a college class in literature to get any critical impression said is another case in point. The noun of quality, though not felt to be an undesirable alien, is not a neighbour to be relied on when wanted. We coax; we suggest; we prod; we perpetually ask, " Why? " Suppose Defoe to be the theme in a class eager to express its amusement at the author's impersonal and unemotional quality. The average student will observe, " Why, I notice the way he narrates without putting in anything he feels." Suppose Spenser the theme in a class keen to note the obvious symbolism of the Una-lion meeting. As Juventus puts it, " The lion bowed down before her and licked her hand as if he recognized in her something superior to himself." Are Chaucer's humane sympathies before us? We are sure to hear of " the way the poet has of laughing at a person without meaning to do him any harm." The speaker has the right " sort of feeling." His heart is commonly in the right place, but the place is certainly not the nexus of intellectual distinctness. Its necessary language is beckoned in:

> " At first it seemed a little cloud,
>   And then it seemed a mist.
> It neared and neared and took at last
>   A certain shape I wist."

But for his part Juventus would be content that the shape should remain permanently a bit uncertain.

Or it would be fairer to say that popular taste really prefers the shadowy idea. We have, many of us, an æsthetic reluctance to the actual definition of a thought, as if it were an indelicacy, as if to call a thought a thought were only less compromising than to call a spade a spade. It seems to violate the privacy of an idea, like a rude rush into a room or the blunt announcement of a portentous circumstance without the tact of social preliminary. We prefer, we say, the nuance to the bold stroke.

III

But with all the assurance we can command from the prophets of the concrete, we must needs remember sometimes with a little misgiving our human reluctance to grow up. The clinging of man through each of the seven ages to the age before is a commonplace of psychology. And to children life is not a thought but a story. Little girls are made, we know, of sugar and spice and all things nice, and the ingredients are for the making of cake. Little boys

are made of bows and arrows and little wheel-
barrows, for the career of the complete Indian. To
the adolescent life very frequently is a sort of description, a more or less sensitive squeezing of
youth's orange to get the greatest quantity of juice,
or as Pater would more elegantly put it, " to get the
greatest number of pulsations into a given time."
The adult is supposed to inherit the power of
thought, though few indeed are the philosophers of
Plato who have beheld the ideas pure, shining in
light.

Newman's notion of culture, " the consciousness
of mental enlargement," is still only half old-fashioned. To our ideal, too, history is not a study of
events but a " conscious superiority over them." The
pitiful among the children of men are still those who
" generalize nothing." " They see the tapestry of human life, as it were on the wrong side, and it tells no
story." The analogy is noble. It were perhaps frivo-
lous to alter it and say rather that they see human
life only as a tapestry in which is woven forever a
story, revealed in a picture of which they propose
to themselves no adequate interpretation. At least to
have only the image and the language of imagery is
" to generalize nothing."

For the evasion of the abstract word in modern
vocabulary is not, one greatly fears, a philosophical
preference of the process to the goal, nor the creative lust of the artist for the word of sense. It is but
the most obvious case of our choice for the way of
least intellectual resistance. Comments have been

made immemorially and brilliantly on the expedients of the human mind to evade a labour. There is no labour which the mind more conscientiously eludes than the labour to corner its notion, to focus the thought into the difficult distinctness of intellectual language, to wrestle with the idea till it gives up its name.

To remember the *mot juste* of thought is no treason to the *mot juste* of sense. We shall never have too keen a relish for concreteness, for the verb direct, for the immediate adjective, for the noun of fact quick with life. But the less accessible language of intellectual differentiation comes by no means "by nature," is quite as much in need of protective cults. Whether is it simpler to name the scents which rise darkling from a June evening or the thoughts which wander through eternity?

And to quicken the dormant "sort of feeling" into tangibility is no less expression, is no less life. For the *mot juste* of thought is the word of realization in which beginnings come to something, the word of concentration in which vagaries draw together, the word of domination in which the thinker becomes "superior to things." To honour it effectually would be to revive a form of artistic consciousness which goes a-begging in a world which yearns fatuously "to express itself"—a form not to be achieved by all the crunchings of all concreteness.

"I came; I saw; I conquered," said Cæsar in verbs. And he chose for himself the best possible sentence structure, since his was a way of doings.

But it is the business of Cæsar's critics more often to name the things which Cæsar saw, the conquests he achieved, to note the causes and the consequences of these sights and deeds, to name the qualities which made Cæsar a comer and a conqueror.

"Arms I sing and the man," said Virgil. And the world is agreed that he wrote very well in his simple nouns. He would assuredly have lost much momentum both in Latin and English if he had related in a tangle of verbs and pronouns, "I sing of how men fought one another in battle and of how one man did more and greater things than another."

"And now abideth faith, hope, love," said another master of strong expressiveness, "and the greatest of these is love." It is a climax to the riot of noble imagery which he has placed before. One might safely challenge anybody to say just this with equal effectiveness in the pictorial but less intellectual language of concrete experience.

VII

THE ESCAPE FROM NARCISSUS

I

I REMEMBER when I first read in a primer of
psycho-analysis that we cling to detective stories because of our secret yearnings for " escape."
For a long time I had evaded extended disquisitions
on the psycho-analyfical theme and had got along at
secondhand, depending upon its reflection in Freud-
ian fiction and in the initiate wits of my glib pupils.
I had managed to shelter my illusions rather well.
The Narcissus of my acquaintance had been that
very nice young man in the Naples museum. Oedipus
had been my idea of human tragedy supreme and
nobly held. The sudden light from the primer's wisdom was a strain upon my mental vision, but I was
pleased to be reassured about my criminal appetites
on such soundly old-fashioned lines.

Only the day before I had been standing with an
academic colleague beside our private little loan col-
lection of novels which the College library obligingly
housed in the basement behind the sign which said,
" Students are not allowed to pass beyond this
point." It was a small affair, but as far as the money
went it was spent to get us precisely what we chose.
There were of course a few bits of antic naughtiness

to give a tone. But the bulk were of the common sort, well-fingered, apt for professorial desire. My colleague and I stood for awhile, looking the offering over. She urged me to read *The Delicate Fiend,* and I pressed upon her *Death in the Egg Cup.* She finally chose *One of us is a Murderer,* and I turned away and sought my home with the *Valley of Creeping Men* tucked under my arm. It would do very well, and furnish forth enough of human nature's daily food to go to sleep on.

Escape to story-book used to be held an alarming proclivity of youth. It was the little boy of Thackeray's roundabout memory who used to end the evening, too amazed to go to bed, with *The One-Handed Monk* or *The Adventures of Corinthian Tom.* It was the Stevenson of " A Penny Plain and Twopence Coloured " who led his happiest hours in fellowship with great-hearted characters who answered to such names as Three-Fingered Jack or The Terror of Jamaica. Of late youth has grown wiser, burdened with literary cares which I, fortunately, am not compelled to share. Grow old along with me. Escape nowadays is for the elderly and unashamed.

And, according to the text-book, I need have no scruples about detective stories. Quite respectable folks, it repeated, might turn to them, not from thwarted instinct for power as I had heard somewhere else, — just through a reasonable wish to be released from reality in tired but harmless hours. I was still safe and sane enough as long as I searched not for the true romance but only for the strictly untrue. And our three small shelves seemed to meet in perfection the requirement of unveracity.

II

We shall never get anything again to rival the mystery story for opiate emptiness. Here is no expression to be puzzled over: here is the expression of just nothing at all. I am rested as by the rush of a fast express whose strong rattle assures me that we have come a long way from the last station and have still a good bit to go before the next. And I know my fellow-passengers so well — those excellent detectives, the strong young man with athletic build and clean-cut chin and clear blue eye, and the oldish man with the humorous mouth who inclines to be plump and looks as if he did nothing but cultivate his garden. I need not say they are both from Scotland Yard.

Scotland Yard I intend never to see, though I understand that it is somewhere near the Strand and not far from that gorgeous Whitehall guard. It is surely small and inconsiderable to the eye, like the Bank of England. It is, I take it, a paved court, roughly stoned, surrounded by strong palisades just above the height of a man's eye. On the four sides thereof are offices, dark, replete with secrets, repositories of impalpable resource.

But the detective story, we fear, is wearing to its end, having exhausted the tale of criminal invention.

We shall not see the like again of that little red insect under excellent stage management, whose barest bite was deadly poison, turned loose at darkest night to seek his straight way to the intended victim. We shall not beat that secret Italian poison which killed at once or after the passage of years as the exigencies of the narrative required. We shall try in vain to parallel the congenial lawyer who in off-hours set explosives diabolically and subterraneously, or the travelling curate expert in cipher who shot diamonds through ventilators, or the butler, super-captain of industry who ruled his gang from the vantage-ground of the pantry. What shall we do without the endless avatars of the German emperor and his subsidiary scientists subtle in electrocution, without the recurrent embroilments of international picking and documentary stealing by a fictitious Bolshevism? And those earlier conceptions provided perfectly the critical satisfactions sanctioned by poetic justice. Witness a notable though forgotten book, wherein all the characters good and bad were assembled in a tower, and straightway all the bad ones blown to bits and all the good ones commodiously protected by architectural pieces of the ruined structure so fallen as to be precisely virtue's guard.

But as the mystery-mongers have anticipated an ultimate downfall of their prestige, they have seemed smitten with a fatal madness which is fast precipitating their end. They are presuming to undermine the conditions and the foundations of their very existence. They have developed a regrettable tendency to take liberties with Scotland Yard. Much may be pardoned to the search for variety. There is a limit to the number of negotiable poisons. Insects which make their exits and their entrances at the proper times and in the desired directions must necessarily be few. It is all very well to murder sporadic policemen pressing too close on a scent too hot. But never should unhallowed hand deface the inviolable precinct. A certain offensive book has already wrought iconoclastic influence on its successors. It has invaded the sacred court. It has sowed death in all the waste-baskets. It poisoned the official inkwells. This was going too far. Scotland Yard must be safeguarded, — today's last sanctuary of pale romance.

III

For the real lure of Scotland Yard has been that here alone in modern book-land I have been sure of never meeting any of those novelists who, like me, have been enormously impressed at some time by a primer of psycho-analysis. Fiction was much more comfortable and satisfactory in the days before the latest fall of man, the most up-to-date discovery of the knowledge of good and evil. To be honest, I should still prefer reality to unreality in fiction if I could get it plain. There used to be other ways of escape.

I myself have another. Luckily, I must spend a large share of my academic hours in the old-fashioned company of Tom Jones, and Roderick Randon, Joseph Andrews, and Peregrine Pickle — and I believe I may say Tristram Shandy too since he never took his obscenities seriously. I never feel uneasy in their company, though their open way is often soiled and the fellowship to which they introduce me is sometimes disreputable and foul enough. I find life in their society singularly free from anxiety. I know exactly where I am without aid of gloss and can interpret for myself their tricks and their manners. I am never for a moment baffled by the Tom Jones stream of consciousness. Never am I at loss, as I follow the page, to distinguish between his acts and his fancies and his feelings, his visual images and his pretences. He is, I admit, conscious of comparatively little; he is for the most part singularly free from such impedimenta as thoughts and fancies. But as far as my author is concerned, I am welcome to know what I am looking at. I may still see my ill-starred Tom, too, according to my old-fashioned liking, in the round. He does not vanish, as he might in a contemporary novel, into his psychology — drowned, as it were, in the stream of his consciousness. My heroes, too, are beastly enough to be at home in any period, but with a consistency and predictability which would put them quite outside the pale of the " incongruity " required by the best people of the present. I meet besides no hard problems of suppression and repression, for my young blades were never known to repress a lust of any sort. And as for Oedipus — when Tom Jones be-

lieved himself for a season to be a very Oedipus, he
was scared well nigh out of his wits by the notion. I
were ungrateful to complain in such company, and
I am far from complaining. But after all it is the
twentieth and not the eighteenth century in which
I live. If I would be in touch with my generation, I
must " back to abnormalcy."

It is the sexuo-psychological enthusiast to whom
I return with most reluctance. And even here I
would not willingly be squeamish. It is always just
as well to know the latest thing in naturalism.

It would be churlish to quarrel, for instance, with
the eternally fleshly school of the eternal adolescent.
" Make me anything but neuter! " is a catch-word of
rejoicing youth, old as the hills, able to take forever
a modern phrasing, healthy and frank enough whatever new code it chooses for its signals, though
wrapped in the latest formulae and tricked in the
nattiest of ultra-devices. That aspiring and radiating
spirit is a sort of virtue as it cries to life, " O, brave
new world that has such sins to sin, such eldorados
to unearth, such forms to smash, such necessities to
ignore, such experience to make us sad."

Nor would I lack respect for the complexities of
our social analysts, who are so busy placing the axe
at the root of the tree. The sexual muddle of a modern world is to them as a matter of course both a
cause and a base conclusion of its corruption, symbol
of an order that is dead, unequal to life, fit only to be
cast into the fire, unless the dry stock conclude to
bud with miraculous promptitude. At least they have

made real work of their bold labour, have woven a
tapestry close-knit and terrible and full, picture of a
society tormented, condemned, beneath the illusion
of its peace and joy. They would take up this old
world and shake it hard to see whether or not it will
hold together, with a special conviction beforehand
that the sawdust will come out and the structure part
asunder. They have my consent. It will come apart
or it will not, and in either case so much the better.
I would only suggest that the ways of prophecy are
cold. I would beg the prophets as a special favour
not to threaten in English. They shall prophesy, and
may do so well, in German, in Russian, or even in
French. But the English novel, which one may still
venture to think well of, has kept its characteristic
offhand ease because it has not been used, whatever
its exterior didacticism, to take itself, its subject or
its form, with the ultimate seriousness.

No, not from youth, and not from the prophet do I
shrink.

But I quail before the novelistic Narcissus, holding in one hand a mirror and in the other his primer
of psychology. He is so worthy and so solemn about
the matter. He pores over his business with a sober
earnestness, narrowing to a brooding page the various book of life. He has read in the writings of
others; he has recorded in his own — that energy
is sex — and echo has replied. And Meredith is dead.
His friends have been till rather lately lapped in
lead. And few are strong enough to declare in fiction
without timidity that other doctrine equally known

to the psychologists — that sex is energy — tidings
not of disgust. It is a message waiting from the past.
But Narcissus is still too rapt to hear anything. That
was a wise old mystic who pointed out centuries ago
that " the Devil too has his contemplatives." Of such
as these there is no weariness. " The Prince of Darkness is a gentleman," with an excellent sense of
humour. But what of the careful, the solemn, contemplative of the flesh?

I tell myself to be of a stout heart. Almost, one
believes, the evangel of sex must have penetrated to
the most remote fastness of provincialism. Already
one sniffs a distinct change in the morning air. But
he waits, meanwhile — the contemplative of the flesh
— cabined in the sunless round of a weary and conscientious prurience.

So come, still come, clean murder, thy sword dripping good red blood! And splendid arson, thou that
dealest with the pure element of fire, itself mag-
nificently stolen from high heaven! White-handed
theft, mercurial, fertile in resource! Be ye my comforts and my visitants, to soothe my pillow and to lull
my sense!

It is the hour. Haply the Queen Moon is on her
throne. Good things of day begin to droop and
drowse. I turn on the reading-lamp. I take up the
book. Before me stands a figure — yes, it is the
athletic young man who is really my favourite, he
of the clean-cut chin and the clear-blue eye. Behind

him opens a lane, long, shadowy at the end. What is that shape lying prone at the turning, with others hurrying in its direction? Yes, it is a prostrate human form, struck down, I have no doubt at all, by a ruffian and mysterious hand. Ah, already with thee!

VIII

CAPS AND BELLS

I wonder that this generation,
So avid for emancipation,
Iconoclastic of intention
Toward tradition and convention,
Lacks resolution to revoke
The domination of the joke.

In social circles everywhere
Motley, we know, 's the only wear.
Popular mode for either sex —
The rattle and the hues duplex,
Those well worn tights of red and yellow,
The coxcomb, badge of Punchinello.
The cap with bells, though fashions veer
Through cycles, bides accepted gear.

Tear, if you will, our fame to tatters,
Only our sense of humour matters.
Our pride, howe'er misfortunes range
Through flood or fire or stock exchange,
Though ruin and disaster take one —
To make a joke, or try to make one.

Of special sanction I would guess
The joke that comes from righteousness.

Religions muscular or mystic
Agree in being hedonistic.
The Collect begs — you'll find it there —
In Liturgy for Common Prayer,
Along our path with dangers rife
God's blessing on a sober life;
But in our modernistic wise,
We'd rather pray, " Let laughter rise! "
And wheresoe'er we look the while,
Is Duty's everlasting smile.

A weary laugh, I undertake,
The laugh that rings for conscience' sake:
Take Rosalind in her distress,
Harrassed by well meant friendliness,
And urged by Celia's kindly folly
To cast away her melancholy,
To furbish up a sparkling glance,
And show a merry countenance.
Her honest answer claims my love:
" I show more mirth than I am mistress of! "
But Celia all the while kept at her
With virtuous, sunshiny chatter,
Till sadly the poor girl awoke
From tears and did her best to joke.
Celia, I swear, and hold my own,
Might well have left the girl alone.

In days of old, young and spontaneous,
They used the joke extemporaneous,

The quip a fine adventure hurled
Into an undiscovered world.
A thing to die for, the *bon mot*
In a good cause, said Cyrano.

Authentic Puck, that sprite of worth,
Could put a girdle round the earth,
And though the housewife might deplore,
Could sweep the dust behind the door,
Blithesome and tricksy, filled with glee
For things which fall preposterously.
He bore good nonsense in his pack,
But modern Puck has lost the knack.
Our comic borders on our tragic.
Whither is fled the fairy magic?

Folly divine, the wits agree,
Courses afield with Liberty,
She wanders light along the mountains,
And drinks of far aerial fountains,
Or follows in an antique dance
The footing of the " True Romance."
Only we know, nor need reminder,
The soul that seeks her shall not find her.

Let us one day take a vacation,
By presidential proclamation,
And, by consent of one and all,
Enjoy a stupid interval.
Doff cap and bells all in a twinkle,
'Twould seem so good to miss their tinkle!

We're very bright, — our friends all know it —
Why take such monstrous pains to show it?
Let's shed by prearrangement fit
The glorious lightning of our wit,
And, to give comfort perfect measure —
Relax the foolish face of pleasure,
Turn down the light, neglect the fire,
Yielding to opiate desire
Till in unconscious, sweet surrender
We put our feet up on the fender;
Then, packed in pillows, doze and mull,
Snug and unconscionably dull.

A dream alas! We should not venture
To face the quiet or the censure.
We should awake, untaught at morning,
Look once about the place with longing,
Cast a sad glance upon the embers
All wistfully as who remembers
How comfortable used to be
The hours of joy, in misery —
Then cry — so habitude compels —
" Fetch me straightway my cap and bells! "